Breakfast on the Patio

By Sheila Douthwaite

Proverbs 3:5-6 'Trust in the Lord with all your heart and lean not on your own understanding; in all your ways acknowledge him, and he will make your paths straight.'

Breakfast on the Patio

Sheila Douthwaite

ISBN: 978-0-9572420-0-5

Second Edition, 2016.

First published, 2012.

Publisher, Busy Corner Books, Lincolnshire.

www.busycornerbooks.com

Front cover picture: The old kitchen and Honeysuckle Cottage. Back cover picture: Mom and dad Silkie hens, brooding a clutch of fertile eggs.

Names and locations have been changed in this book to protect identity.

Some details have been changed for entertainment purposes.

Do you enjoy writing?

<u>Fantastic</u> new motivational book/note pad now available in paperback format, see www.busycornerbooks.com:

Contents

2006-2016

Dedication

Never have I loved a man so much in all my life. Without his support and encouragement I somehow don't think I would have got through this surreal life changing experience. For that, Frank, I thank you.

To our most precious Maggie, darling, we love you so very much.

Mum and Dad, for all the times you could have said,

'I told you so!', but didn't. God bless you.

*

Thank you to Lincolnshire Poacher Magazine for publishing our article, An Inspiring Lincolnshire Cottage, in your 2012 summer issue. Thank you to Lincolnshire Life Magazine, The Writers Magazine, Lincolnshire Echo Newspaper, Louth Leader Newspaper and Skegness Standard for writing about our city to countryside transformation.

In memory of our lovely Garfield look-a-like
cat, Fudge. 1998-2010

Rose-tinted glasses –
our very own escape to the country
2006

Surrounding fields.

Frank worked very hard at his job for years and years and achieved great skills as a carpenter 'on the tools'. However, a career change in the 1990s led him to study a more holistic lifestyle. This was around the time we first met. Both studying psychotherapy and trying to discover our true selves through dissecting our personal histories, we also loved being close to nature and felt inspired by the natural things in life. After my divorce, our friendship grew into a loving relationship. It was like being given another chance to be a real family again. I could sell my house. Maggie, my fifteen-year-old daughter, and I, could move in with Frank and then he could sell his too. Then, we could buy our dream country cottage together and do our best to live happily ever after. It didn't matter that we were in our mid-forties - we could still live the 'good life!'. I conveniently forgot about the chronic pain that had been with me since having several abdominal operations, and how I fought each day to keep up with even simple tasks, like cleaning and cooking. I decided my life was not over yet, it was only just beginning – there were so many more adventures in store. You see, Frank was brought up to be independent from a very young age, although this led to him 'doing his own thing' somewhat, like purposely missing the school bus to light fires and make tree swings. From a 1970s youth of swimming in the overflow from Leeds's Robin Hood lead works instead of going to school, to making a top notch tree swing which, in his own words, 'felt like it swung a hundred feet into the air.' Young Frank had quite an independent and colourful time. But the grown-up Frank taught me such a lot. One, to let my hair down, and two, to enjoy the moment - live life as if no one is watching. So I did, we all did...

It was when I had a moment of madness whilst having a clear out at home one day. I came across a gift Mum and Dad gave me for my twenty-first birthday. It was a Royal Albert plate showing a Victorian lady standing below an arched trellis and in the background, a fairy-tale cottage in a lovely green grassy meadow. 'How lovely' I remarked to Frank. 'Wouldn't it be nice if..., just think, eh?' Frank would often joke and say that I looked at the world through rose-tinted glasses and all I ever wanted was a gingerbread cottage with roses around the door. With my naivety and enthusiasm, I could dream away. There was nothing wrong with dreaming and it wasn't harming anyone. But the moments of madness continued when Frank decided to take me seriously. We started to meet on a regular basis to discuss possibilities, and make lists and plans of what we all wanted for our future. Very sensible really, considering that the overall decision was to move to somewhere we knew very little about. We had driven through villages on day trips to the Lincolnshire coast. The house prices were cheaper than our home town of Leeds and Wakefield in Yorkshire, and the Lincolnshire countryside was well known for having fertile land: ideal for our own 'good-life'.

So I don't know whether logic disappeared as we put on those rose-tinted glasses or whether we were just living life for the moment, but we decided to move in together and then plan our very own escape-to-the-country. Obviously, we discussed our plans with Maggie and she was a little defensive at first, but soon settled to the idea. Frank and I wanted to give her the best possible chance to live a healthy and happy life, away from all the muck and grime of the city. Consequently, the poor girl learned all about very early starts with long country journeys to and from college. After our move, we had to get up around 5.50 a.m. on weekdays. After breakfast we would drive Maggie to the next village where a bus would pick her up at 7.15 a.m. Her study day would start around 9 a.m. and I would pick her back up from the bus stop at around 6 p.m. We got home at around 6.30 p.m., and after tea, Maggie then had homework to complete. She soon had enough of trying to stay awake during studies at her new college, and left to find work in a nearby town. She did however make lots of friends very quickly, and found the all-important new boyfriend.

For the first eighteen months, Frank still worked at his job in a Leeds high school. He commuted there on a Sunday evening, stayed with friends and came back home on Thursday morning. Weekends and term time were taken up with the renovation work to our new countryside home, and trying to find other ways to earn money to pay for the unexpected surprises in store. Perhaps most people would find work in their desired location and then move to the area. Maybe our idea was a strange way around, but we chose to make our dream happen instead of hoping for something to turn up. Two years after moving to Lincolnshire and after much searching, we eventually found Frank another job in a nearby town.

Writing this book has been a blessing in getting me through the emotional changes of moving from the bustling cities of Leeds and Wakefield to a calm, serene countryside cottage-in-the-middle-of-nowhere location in Lincolnshire. A place where you could easily start and talk to the animals because there is no one else nearby. I convey great respect to local folk who have grown up in a rural environment, because it takes a different kind of strength to live a full life in the rural countryside when you have always been used to living in a modern, very clean house, that is free of spiders, flies and dust.

There are probably lots of would-be renovators who would not dream of buying a project and living in the same house at the time of continuing building works. I guess most would buy a caravan, live in it for a short while, until their house became habitable. However, we didn't have that luxury because our money soon disappeared into the bottomless pit. Madness drove us to purchase our Honeysuckle Cottage without a detailed homebuyers survey. We subsequently discovered damp, cracks and all sorts of interesting necessities for our attention.

We were faced with no choice, in order to make the house into a comfortable, healthy, safe environment, we had to work – at a tremendous cost to our sanity and well-being.

Ongoing notes and drafts, along with obsessive tick lists of jobs to do each day for our new home, have been piled up on our bedside table ever since we first moved here. It has taken lots and lots of hard work and dedication to get where we are today. Please do not be offended by any of the comments I make; they are merely written to give you a sense of our reality here at Honeysuckle Cottage. This is the place where writing lists and ticking each item off became a near obsession and paranoia crept into our overtired lives. We fell over badgers in our garden at night and climbed forty-foot apple trees to rescue our cat. We cleaned out our septic tank to get the pipes flowing again and learned all about keeping hens and ducks, as well as growing our own fruit and vegetables. We learned how to use a gun and we wore woollen hats and scarves in bed during wintertime. We renovated our garden and encouraged its wildlife, whilst Frank touched every single part of this house to make Honeysuckle Cottage our home. We lost contact with many friends and relatives back in Yorkshire. However, we have also met lots of wonderful people along our way. On many occasions we have shared tea and cakes whilst watching the world pass us by with neighbours who lost their dog down a badger hole, farmers who delivered feral chickens, electricians who needed our help, plumbers who preferred to sit and chat, telephone engineers frightened of mice, aerial contractors afraid of heights, parcel delivery people who needed a break, the vicar who didn't believe in God, and the one and only Mother Nature who brings such beauty into our garden.

This book may make you smile or even laugh out loud; it could make you cry. There are one or two places, for those who have a sensitive heart, where you may cringe at the stomach-churning events or even shiver at some of the things we did to get through. However, I tell you our story as it is, to give you a sense of what life is really like here. I am not a seasoned writer and my grammar may not be quite perfect, I just want to share our story with you. There are one or two names and places that I have changed to protect identities. However, all the events are true. I do hope you enjoy reading our book.

Viewing day
Late May 2007

Longs Lane, leading to Honeysuckle Cottage.

Let me tell you about the viewing day, the time we went to see our wonderful Honeysuckle Cottage. We drove into the village and took a turning right and over an old railway bridge. The road then changed from two lanes to a single track road, but still tarmacked. There was an old railway house on the right and fields all around. The road was winding and single track all the way. We passed another cottage in the middle of a field and a farm on our right. Chickens in a field seemed to belong to a great big hen house sited on our right. We continued on the windy road for around a mile until we saw a leaded church steeple, rising above the other houses in the village ahead. We drove up and around the church, passing a farm on the right, and turned right at a little junction. There, straight in front of us, was a beautiful village green with trees growing all around. There were houses on the right and another farm set back on a hill. Then more houses appeared to lead around a corner and into the village. However, on our left was the sign for Longs Lane. This was it: Honeysuckle Cottage was up there somewhere in the distance. We drove along Longs Lane and past the farm, past another small cottage – then the road ended! We looked straight ahead at a long, uneven single track lane with huge potholes, with only fields in the distance. The track was long and straight. There was a dead end sign, but we knew the cottage was up there somewhere because the estate agent told us it was.

We put the car into first gear and drove gently along this dusty, bumpy and stony surface. For around a quarter of a mile we listened to the grass in the middle of the lane scraping on the bottom of our car - we looked at each other and cringed, followed by a childish excited smile.

In the distance, we could see trees which seemed to reach high into the sky. They surrounded something on the right hand side. Was this it? Yes, it was, because as we approached, the vendors were standing at the open five-bar gate and gestured us onto the grass bank at the side of a five-foot dyke. The man was standing there holding what looked like a long walking stick, just as tall as him. He held it like a weapon to warn off unwanted visitors. He wore a cowboy hat with pheasant feathers threaded through it. We just smiled and dismissed it as eccentricity. His wife dashed out to greet us - she wore a green gingham checked pinafore with splash marks of what I imagined were possibly from home-made strawberry jam – she had pink rosy cheeks and a welcome smile. We pulled onto the grass verge and got out of the car. The sun was shining in a beautiful clear blue sky and birds were singing. It was as if we had landed in the Garden of Eden: the peace, the quiet, the wonder of it all. The vendors went to sit on an ornamental garden bench at the side of their wooden fence adjoining their chicken coop. Fields surrounded this haven. As we walked up the grass driveway, being careful not to trip in the huge tyre-sized holes made in the ground by the vendor's camper van, just around the corner, we were greeted by the estate agent stood outside the cottage door. We couldn't help but look past him and with wide open eyes and scan the beautiful cottage garden. Honeysuckle Cottage was hiding a huge garden around the back of the property. Oh my goodness, the house viewing had to wait. We just had to walk straight into the garden and so we literally pushed the estate agent out of the way. It's quite difficult to describe; it's one of those instances where you just needed to be there to really appreciate what I am about to tell you. As we left the vendor and the estate agent behind, we walked around the garden. The boundaries of this haven were protected by tall sycamore, oak and willow trees. Hawthorn, sloe, apple and plum trees filled the hedges and corners. The garden was in full flower, I mean all of it; the flowers sparkled and bloomed. A giant wood gazebo covered with honeysuckle, clematis and roses overlooked a large pond at the back of the cottage. Blackbirds and wood pigeons bathed at the waters edge and blue dragon flies glided around like fairies.

Just as an aside, let me tell you about a place near York, called Sutton Hall. The old hall is not a traditional grand heritage house; it is quite natural and almost unkempt. The gardens are very natural and comforting. There are old stone walls with moss growing on them and ornamental figures which are not quite perfect. The flowers are beautiful in the summertime and the insects and birds are amazing. The one thing I remember are the bright blue dragonflies flying around the pond-side. When we lived in Yorkshire, we loved to visit and sit there with our picnic and just soak up the atmosphere. Well, Honeysuckle Cottage garden was very much like that; we were really taken in. This was just the perfect garden, and although the house was also wonderful, without the beauty of Mother Nature, it would be just about nothing; the house and its garden needed and complemented each other.

After those initial breath-taking minutes, we were led into the kitchen through a double stable-style door. The first thing I noticed was the original kitchen sink in the corner. 'Wow', I thought and then ... there were implements hanging from the ceiling and old pictures on the wall and shelves with lines and lines of jam jars with different labels. I was starting to feel ever so excited.

Frank was brandishing the list we had carefully put together of all the things a house needed for us to say yes. I could hear the paper start to rustle and crumble as we ignored it. My imagination got the better of me. The floor boards lay uncovered, but protected by huge woollen rugs. The walls had wallpaper with a huge fruit pattern. The ceiling was low and had an exposed beam.

There was a cooker under the chimney breast and two large chunky pine dining tables filled most of the floor, with two tapestry and leather chairs sharing the remainder. There was a country-green washed pine sideboard and tall free-standing food cupboards; just lovely. Already in my head, I could see myself as Ma Larkin, waltzing around the kitchen and making all those things that Mum and Nanna had taught me all those years ago. I couldn't wait. I felt like skipping, my feet were floating – or was I becoming quite neurotic, who knows?

We were led through the kitchen and into the living room. Old double wooden glass-panelled doors were wide open and showed a wonderful view of the huge garden and pond. The living room had an old leather and tapestry sofa and dominating the room was a pine fireplace with a cast iron support, indicating the potential for an open fire. More old pictures decorated the walls. Again the floor was made of pine floorboards with a lovely woollen countryside scene rug.

The estate agent led us into the downstairs bathroom. We had to duck first through one five-foot doorway and go through a little storage area under the stairs, resembling a pantry with lines of bottles and jars on the shelves, then go through another five-foot doorway and into the bathroom – which had a cast iron bath with old pot sink and toilet. Wow! The floor in the pantry area and downstairs bathroom was small red square quarry tiled. We went back through the doors and into the kitchen, where there was another five-foot doorway, this time leading to a twisting and uneven stairway with no banister. The stairs were barely wide enough to climb up, and that was it – forget about getting any furniture up there. Oh, but the romance of it, so quaint. At the top of the stairs was a two-foot-square platform landing with two ten-inch-high steps leading into each bedroom. The first bedroom we saw was the attic room with a sloping roof. At a squeeze this was just big enough for Maggie. It had the original wide floorboards and a small single glazed window. The main bedroom had been divided to provide an old wooden clothes cupboard and an en suite with shower. Again it had the original polished floorboards and the bedroom itself sloped downwards towards the window by about eight inches. It was like standing in one of those 'houses of fun' at the fairground with the uneven floors. We certainly acted as if we had just finished a fairground ride because all our logic disappeared into the ether. 'Yes, we'll buy it. The asking price, yes, more, yes!' What had happened to us? Did the country air really take its hold? Or was it madness? How were we going to tell

Maggie? What about Mum and Dad and Nanna? Never mind, this was our dream. It was clean, healthy and wonderful – a fantastic opportunity for Maggie to grow up in a clean and fresh environment.

Preparing to move home
Late May 2007

Frank was very busy working in a school as a Youth Counsellor whilst studying at university in his little spare time. I was finishing off my written work for a college course and Maggie was completing her exams and getting ready to leave school, and all her friends. We were exciting about moving to Lincolnshire, we wanted the peace and quiet of rural life and eagerly awaited our completion date and contracts to be exchanged on Frank's house - everything seemed to be running smoothly. We only had two or three people look around before it was sold. We could tell with one couple that they were interested, but the woman was a real battle-axe; she was going to reduce the price by any means, and the estate agent was on the phone with a list of demands from her and a knock-down figure for the house. Cheeky really, but that's the way the market goes sometimes.

Frank had enough to think about so he asked me to arrange for the removal people to give us a quote. We looked together through the telephone directory and saw someone who advertised having years of removal experience and the advertisement was not too big, suggesting that maybe they had a tight budget, like us. 'Hopefully it won't be too pricey' we thought, so I rang and arranged for them to call.

Lots of things were already packed. In Frank's garage, all Maggie's and my belongings were still carefully sealed up from moving out of our bungalow. I supposed this would make it easier for a quote and there was no point in Maggie and me unpacking for the six months we were to spend living here with Frank.

(Looking back, Frank's home in Wakefield was such a homely place. It was a three storey Georgian-style house, built in the late 1980s. There was laminate flooring in the living areas and a warm pastel-coloured carpet upstairs and in the bedrooms too. It was double glazed throughout and centrally heated. For the short time we lived there together, it was easy to maintain and keep clean. But no, we had the wonderful dream of living closer to nature and taking Maggie to a kinder climate with no pollution and fewer people.)

So, there was a knock at the door, the removal man had called to give us a quote for taking all our belongings to Lincolnshire. He must have been in the house for three minutes at the most; rubbing his stubbly chin, he flew in and out of each room saying 'mmm' and 'yes' with a knowing look.

'Yes we can do this, no probs' he said. 'Don't worry lass, you just make sure you got t' kettle on. We've two vans but'll do our best t' just use one'. And that was that.

I felt everything was sorted and proud that I had arranged this all by myself whilst Frank was busy working.

Whilst the sale was proceeding, we had several overnight visits to Lincolnshire and stayed in a few bed and breakfast places. It was all exciting; a new life was starting to appear in front of our eyes. Frank had spent months and months searching the internet and keeping an eye on our favourite cottages for sale. Let me tell you about this particular one. Gosh, it was lovely: it was a beautiful country cottage in a village called New York. It was for sale whilst Frank's was also on the market and we tried to go and view the property. It was two old red brick cottages knocked through to make one. There was a patio, much like that of a manor house, at the front and then some grand steps with big stone bowls at each side leading to a huge lawn. In the distance, there were two large poly tunnels and a paddock. Wonderful! In the property particulars the house looked charming inside, with many original features; the only thing which put us off was the electric heating and that it only had a shower room, not a bath. (It makes me laugh now when I think of those two little minor details; when I consider all the work we have carried out here at Honeysuckle Cottage, putting in a new bathroom would have been child's play. But, as I am told very often by Frank, our renovation project is all 'character building!')

Even though our sale in Wakefield was going through rather quickly, by this time, so was this cottage in New York, but we still kept an eye on things. We really liked this place and each time we visited Lincolnshire our journey included a quick drive past to check on whether it was back on the market. In fact, even when we found our Honeysuckle

Cottage and the process was going through with the solicitors, we went to New York – to the property itself. Now, I realise this is something which could have seemed a little pushy, but we thought we would just see if their sale was still going through all right. Frank and I pulled up at their five-bar gate and wondered whether to go any further into the garden as it felt a little private. However, Frank being the person he is, he went and knocked at the door – no reply. He waited a while and then he shrugged his shoulders and I gestured to him through the car window to come back to the car. It looked like there was no one home. Frank was just about to get back into his seat when a red-faced, middle-aged man appeared from inside one of the poly tunnels. He was wearing bedraggled clothes and was carrying a gun.

'Yup,' he said.

'Erm, hello there, sorry to bother you, but is your house still sold because we really love it?'

'Yup,' he said, raising his gun a little.

We even asked if we could have a look around, and by this time I had got out of the car, but his wife was fast approaching the gate, brush in hand. The message got through; she didn't want us around and frowned at our presence. We apologised and got back into the car. Oh well, it was not to be and it was just one of those things. We should probably have accepted it had sold. However, we did ring the estate agent and gave our telephone number so they could let us know if the sale fell through. Not that the owners would want us to buy their beautiful cottage anyway. It was, after all, a little rude of us town folk to bother their peaceful lives.

Willoughby Woods, near Alford.

Moving day
Late July 2007

Moving day was 26th July 2007. We were as organised as possible, with boxes packed up in each room. I had the kettle on, waiting for the removal people to arrive. I looked through our bay window to see oily smoke clouds spurting out of the exhaust of an old rusty white box van with about six people squashed into the front. They had arrived to move the precious contents of our home! Frank had a right tantrum, as foul words flew out of his mouth. 'I can't look, how on earth are they gonna get all this in there, without breaking something?' The van was only thirteen feet long by seven feet high and six feet wide. I just took a deep breath and totally detached myself from the situation – there was nothing we could do about it now but imagine how many things might get broken if the van burst open on the motorway. But, much to our surprise, the removal people drank their tea as they raced around in an organised fashion, with a big, fat leader who sorted out what went where. He certainly knew his job. I know we didn't have much, but they managed to organise all our belongings, everything, and pack it neatly into the one van and get it to Honeysuckle Cottage safely. The weirdest thing was they didn't have satellite navigation, we lost them on the motorway and yet they managed to get there before we did. Strange to say the least.

The day we moved in it teemed down with rain all day. Flash flooding was terrible, especially in nearby villages and in the towns of Louth and Horncastle. Water had run off from the Wolds and flooded people's homes, causing havoc in people's lives. We heard on the news on the radio of how people from places like Wainfleet and Boston had to be evacuated because of the floods. Also the River Witham had burst its banks, causing the same distress for many people. It certainly tested our dykes around the cottage and garden, but we didn't flood at all. (There are five-foot drains running parallel along both sides of Longs Lane, each one joining the main twenty-foot drain which takes any surplus water to the sea – about ten miles away). Longs Lane was particularly waterlogged, with the potholes full to the brim. However, Honeysuckle Cottage's drainage system, tested to its limits, worked very well.

On the day we moved in I took a video with my mobile phone (if you would like to watch it, search on internet on You Tube for Frank Douthwaite Moving Home July 2007) and managed to catch the back of fifteen-year-old Maggie with her waterproofs on as she walked around the garden. She was holding her hood with both hands and squinting through the rain drops as she slowly turned and seemed to look around in horror at all the vegetables, fruit trees, greenhouses, summer houses, and runner beans filling half the view. I guessed she may have been wondering where the local shops or youth club were, when in fact the nearest building to hold a social occasion was the village hall three miles away. Oh my, what had we done? All she could see were cows and fields in the distance - poor Maggie!

Our new home
August 2007

Working in a full circle, I am going to describe each room in our cottage, starting from the main entrance door. As you follow us around, we will then guide you from the cottage into our wonderful quarter acre garden. This is just how we experienced Honeysuckle Cottage when we had travelled, fully laden with our belongings, from Yorkshire to Lincolnshire on that rainy July afternoon.

Honeysuckle Cottage was built sometime between 1850 and 1890. It is a brick construction, and is now cement rendered, painted magnolia. In the past fifteen to twenty years, two extensions have been added: a room currently used as a dining area (with the main entrance door to the cottage) and a downstairs bathroom to the side (accessed internally, through a walk-in pantry area under the stairs, inside the original kitchen area). Both have pitch roofs with concrete tiles that match the original property. The cottage has two bedrooms and oil-fired central heating, and it is connected to the mains water supply. Toilet waste flows out of the cottage, through drains and into an underground old cast-iron septic tank filtering system. Once the water has been filtered, it flows through pipes and into a four foot dyke to the lane side. Other waste water from the washing machine, shower and sink, flows straight out and into this same dyke. Any soap, shampoos, cleaners, disinfectants and washing powders have to be environmentally friendly, so they do not harm any plants or wildlife.

The cottage has mains electricity, but no telephone connection and there is no TV aerial.

The cottage is built on a clay foundation. Many houses were built on clay during the Victorian and Edwardian times. (We were told by a surveyor that if the house had poor foundations and was going to move at all, it would have done so by now, so we gave a sigh of relief at this and took the man at his word.) When built originally, it possibly had four outbuildings. Presently, only two remain. There is a wash house on your left, next to the perimeter hedges and near the entrance gate. It is approximately eleven feet long by seven feet wide. The other outbuilding is an outside privy or toilet (now used for storing tools) to the right and around twenty yards away from the cottage door. Once owned by local farmers, the cottage was originally built for farm workers and their families to live in whilst they worked in the fields and it was later inherited by or sold on to other local landowners. In those days many local families, including their young children, still worked in the fields, digging, seeding, harvesting and ploughing. Less than thirty years ago, the farmer and his family who own the twenty-acre fields surrounding Honeysuckle Cottage would still weed their crops by hand, although in recent years the fields have been used as grazing land for cattle and sheep.

As you walk through the wooden stable-style entrance door you go straight into the dining area. This is one of the extensions, built around fifteen years ago on the side of the original cottage – it fits very well and adds to the character of the old place. It is thirteen feet by eleven feet, a good-sized room with two windows on your left, overlooking fields, and one on your right, beside the entrance door, with a side view of the garden. All three window frames are softwood and stained dark brown, and their surface has been finished off with some kind of implement to create a kind of woodgrain effect on the inside of the frame. Each double-glazed glass panel has water condensation droplets inside its casement, meaning that the seals have deteriorated and need replacing. Looking through the windows, you can see the external frames and sills are quite rotten in places; there are quite a few holes where the wood has broken up. Frank realises these frames need replacing at some point, but they can be made good for the time being with a little wood filler and a thick coat of weatherproof paint.

The dining area has William Morris 'Pomegranate' wallpaper, with a pattern of large oranges, lemons, peaches and pomegranates. There are holes of various sizes in the wall where pieces of attached furniture, like shelves and pictures, have now been removed. The internal woodwork and skirting is all softwood. Again, it has been given a dark woodgrain effect – it looks a bit like thin dark brown and white stripes along each part of the wood. Even the white plug sockets (three sets in all) are painted in this way to make them look like wood. It appears that at some time, someone planned to have a kitchen in this area, because the plug sockets are waist high. Also, two of the windows are in just the right place to give a view of the open farmland, and there is so much more height and light to work and cook in this area. Enquiries have revealed that at one time the cottage did have a kitchen here, but it was taken out by a previous occupier in an attempt to try and make the house more 'in keeping' with an old country cottage.

The floor in the dining area has a huge bare patch in the middle – about eight feet by four feet. This is where there was a large rug. A previous occupier had again painted a woodgrain effect on the chipboard flooring to make it look like old floorboards, but had only painted up to and around their rug. The floor in the dining area is what is technically referred to as a floating floor. A floating floor is usually built on top of a solid concrete base. Basically, it insulates and keeps out the damp. Firstly, large sheets of thin polystyrene are laid onto the floor, followed by a complete covering of plastic damp-proof membrane and then eight-foot-by-two-foot tongue and groove wooden sheets. The wooden sheets are glued together but not fixed downwards. When the glue has dried, the edges are covered and fixed with the skirting board (if skirting is to be fitted) to keep it tight. This kind of floor only looks effective if there is a good solid base and it is fairly level. The dining area floor is quite level, but the skirting board is not fixed properly in many places.

There is a huge black metal chandelier-style light fitting, much like the ones you might find in an old chapel, at the side of a loft hatch. The pointed bottom of this light fitting is only five feet from the floor – watch your head! This roof space is the size of the dining area, it is the loft above this particular extension. The loft is insulated with a few small thin pieces of insulation scattered about here and there.

In the right-hand corner of this dining area, an airing cupboard, with a wooden brace and ledge door, houses the oil-fired central heating boiler.

Running between the dining area and the old kitchen area, just below ceiling height, is a large one-foot-square exposed beam: it divides both rooms in this open plan space. If you are over five feet seven inches tall you need to duck down to pass into the old kitchen, which is in the original part of the cottage.

This old kitchen is eleven feet by nine feet. If you like old-fashioned life, you will instantly fall in love with this special part of the cottage – although it is not very practical. In a small alcove on your left, there is a little cream one-foot-by-two-foot original Belfast sink, an old brass water tap and a solid oak wood drainer of equal age. Just above the sink, there is a two-foot-square, single-glazed and softwood-framed window that overlooks the entrance door to the brick-built washhouse and the gravelled path leading to it. (This window is fastened to the house with bent-over small steel pins on the outside and can be lifted out of its casement.) Here, at head height, a wooden draining rack is attached to the wall, and underneath the sink are very small home-made wooden cupboards painted light green. Opening the doors of these cupboards you can see a soil floor with one or two inlaid bricks and open brickwork to the outside wall. You can't store anything in these cupboards unless you don't mind it being shared with creatures from the garden.

Immediately on the right, next to the sink area and underneath the chimney breast, is the cooker, with a quarry tiled shelf all the way around to hold it in place. As you put your head under the chimney and look upwards, you can see how it has been closed off with a wooden board and that a square has been cut out of the middle and covered with metal gauze to let steam and smoke escape. An exposed beam runs right across this wall, with aged wooden shelves continuing around the adjoining walls. These have potential to be filled with all those jars of home-made jam and chutney. The beams and shelves have old brass hooks to hang bunches of dried herbs, like lavender, sage, thyme, rosemary and mint – all waiting to be picked from Honeysuckle Cottage garden. Fixed to the six-foot-high ceiling in the kitchen is a four-foot-long glaring fluorescent light covered with lace netting that is fastened on with elastic. Behind you, all along the full length of the back wall, original wooden panelling with a beautiful rich old pine colour adds to a cosy atmosphere. The kitchen area is so quaint: the pot sink, small doorways and open beams are rather like a fairy-tale dream – like a magical Grandma's house from childhood, with her amazing and interesting cupboards and all different labelled jars and containers. In reality, however, the old kitchen is small and dark – it has rising damp in the walls, and a sand and soil floor barely covered with small pieces of very uneven red brick setts with the loose and crumbling remnants of cement between them. Like engineering bricks, red brick setts are waterproof and strong; they are half the thickness of a standard size brick, but should still be thick enough to stop damp getting through. Usually, a base of sand is put on top of soil and once both layers have been levelled, the brick setts are laid and fixed together with cement. The cement between the brick setts in the kitchen needs replacing, and quite a few could do with being taken up and straightened. Just imagine trying to make a family meal using a two-foot-square pine table as a workspace in the middle of a kitchen lit by a flickering fluorescent light, bumping your head on the 'aged wooden beam' every time you stir a pan on the cooker, being careful not to trip over and trying to avoid all the spiders and beetles frequenting the sink area when you wash up. However, this still doesn't stop it from looking magical – impractical, yes, but very, very magical.

Three doors lead off the kitchen. The first is into the living room, the second is through a pantry area under the stairs that leads into the downstairs bathroom, and the third is up the winding cottage stairs into the two bedrooms.

All the internal doors are wooden farmhouse ledge and brace. They have large gaps below and above, ranging from two to six inches. The frames are a peculiar size and vary quite a lot, however, they average around two feet six inches wide and five feet six inches high. So, if you are less than five feet six, you are just about OK to walk through quite comfortably. But Frank is six feet two and I am five feet seven. Just imagine the 'fun' we are going to have trying not to bump our heads. For the first few months of living here, you would really need to concentrate when walking through the doorways in the cottage – they could be a hazard if you don't concentrate. The last thing you need to happen - for example, if the telephone rings - is to dash from one part of the cottage to the other, getting a hard smack on the forehead that knocks you to the ground in a daze. But, given time, perhaps five years, I think your backs may be a little arched and you may even duck down through most entrance doorways wherever you go, just through force of habit.

Let us now take a look at the living room – it's through the first door next to the aged wooden shelves in the kitchen area. Watch your head!

This room is thirteen feet by twelve feet. Straight in front of you, through some very old wooden double doors, each with ten glass panels, the cottage's breathtaking country garden and pond is in full view. On a hot summer's day, you could open these doors wide and feel like you were sitting in the middle of the garden. It is so peaceful and tranquil – the only noises you can hear are birds singing, and that's it! Nothing else at all: no traffic, no people, no airplanes. Oh, there is no lock on these doors!

This living room has a cosy feel. It has an open fire, with a pine surround and a burgundy-tiled late Edwardian iron hob grate. The pine surround has three inset wooden panels – one set in the middle and one at either side. We think these may have been fixed at a later date to cover damage or something. However, they are still in keeping with the theme of a country cottage. The six burgundy tiles at each side of the grate are probably not original, and although they have been carefully matched together, the cast-iron hob grate is a little ornate for a country cottage. But it is still aesthetically pleasing and a grand centre piece. Just above the pine surround, on the chimney breast, there is a very old wooden beam – we think this could have been part of the original fireplace.

The walls in the living room are very bumpy and uneven, as would be expected for an old cottage of this age, and they are washed with a magnolia-coloured emulsion. There are a few damp patches above the chimney breast – we presume this could be from soot or muck at the top somewhere or maybe rain getting through during the recent wet weather.

The living room has a floating floor, just like the kitchen, but with stripped pine wooden floorboards instead of boarding. The floor is reasonably level, but the skirting board has not been fitted properly to the walls; it is loose in many places, with pieces missing.

If you like the idea of rural living and the essence of a Victorian era, Honeysuckle Cottage certainly offers a feeling of comfort and warmth, just like a pleasant dream. It is so very different to the stress of living in a city or living in a home where you can hear the neighbours walking up the stairs, opening and closing their doors or flushing their toilet.

Speaking of toilets, let us find the downstairs bathroom –
back out of the living room and into the kitchen. Door
number two is right next to the living room door and this
one leads to an understairs walk-through shelved cold
pantry area. As you bend down to go into this area, you will
see two rows of small narrow shelves attached to the wall at
head level and going all the way around. On your right,
underneath the stairs, are more little shelves and below
them is a storage space around three feet square, again
paved with uneven red brick setts. There is probably
enough space here to put a small fridge or freezer. It feels
quite cool here too and if you switch the light off, it is pitch
black, so maybe it could be useful for storing potatoes,
vegetables or fruits from the garden.

Strange as it may seem, as you stand in this very small area,
just three feet in front of you is another door into the
bathroom. It is a little awkward, but if you bend down and
twist a little, you can get through quite comfortably without
bumping your head on the five-foot-high door frame. So,
you have walked from the kitchen, through a doorway into
the understairs pantry, then through another small door and
are now standing in the downstairs bathroom.

The bathroom is another extension, built around twenty
years ago. The ceiling slopes from four feet at its lowest
point to nearly seven feet where it joins the house. There is
a small two-foot-square window in the corner, on your right.
It has an old, very plain cast-iron rolled top bath, six feet
long, that has been newly enamelled. (We are not sure

where this is from, but it is quite old. Originally, we thought it was possibly 1930s. However, the taps are placed inside and not on top of the bath and after researching and asking around, we think it is from around the early 1900s.) On your left, there is an old Standard toilet (Standard is the manufacturer's name) with an absolutely excellent flush, and a large, old ACI Stonite Ware square pot sink, on your right. The floor in the bathroom is of red quarry tiles. The walls are wood panelled, painted light green.

If you turn around to walk out of the bathroom, through those two doors and back into the kitchen area, around four feet away, on the same wall, but separated by the deep pine wooden panelling, is the third door out of the kitchen, leading up the stairs.

You need to open this small door really fully before you can get through it and up the winding stairs. It is quite a tight spot and you will need to twist, turn and bend to get through there, because of the five-foot-high entrance to the stairwell and then a sharp ninety degrees turn. This is another 'quaint' part of the cottage – the stairs! You may need to grab the step in front of you to get up them and the head height wooden perimeter shelving to get back down again. There are ten steep steps to the top. There is no hand rail, only uneven magnolia-painted walls. The stairs are painted white, up to where a carpet and runners were once fitted, and then they are bare wood with holes where the carpet has been removed. Be careful of the third step: with any weight, it creaks really loudly and feels a little unsafe –

Frank will need to replace this at some point. There is no room here to bring furniture up the stairs; an old cast-iron bed is a possibility, but only if you take it to pieces first and then carry it up bit by bit. A double mattress would be a real test; in fact it could take the best part of a day to get it into the main bedroom, as you push it inch by inch, and it bends, gets stuck and knocks paint from the wall.

At the top of the stairs, as you stand on the two-foot-square landing, the main bedroom is straight in front of you and just above the living room. The room is twelve feet by eleven feet and still has the original fourteen-inch-wide worn rich pine floorboards. The walls are painted bright turquoise and the ceiling has access to the loft above the original cottage – at some time in the past, straw has been used for insulation in the roof space (this will need clearing out and insulating fully). As you stand here, you can't help but notice how the whole room seems to slope down towards the window by a few inches. There is nothing wrong in this; it all just adds to the character. The single-glazed old wood-framed window overlooks the garden, the pond and adjoining farmland – on a clear day, you can see for miles. The wood around the window casement is really quite rotten – there are holes and pieces missing.

This room is partitioned with pine cladding, to make a walk-in wardrobe and an en suite along the outside gable wall. All the woodwork is painted white and the en suite has another brace and ledge door. There is a white fully tiled shower cubicle with a brass showerhead – the shower has a magnificent flow of water. Next to the shower is a very small oval sink and in the corner of this two-foot-by-four-foot space is the Saniflow toilet. It could prove to be a little difficult getting yourself dry from a shower here if the door is closed – you may bump your head on the low ceiling or need to sit on the toilet with the lid down to dry your feet. It may be a good idea to remove this door, to allow a little breathing space in here.

Back onto the landing, to your right, is the small bedroom. It is above the kitchen area and is around eleven feet by eight feet. It also still has the original floorboards. This room has a small wooden and rotting single-glazed window overlooking the wash house, the lane and the fields beyond. It has two small home-made fitted single wardrobes at each side of the room, leaving space for a single bed. These wardrobes are not deep enough to fit coat or clothes hangers; you may find the door will not shut if you try and hang up clothes in there. The walls in this room are uneven and painted with yellow emulsion. There are stencilled patterns of flowers dotted about the walls and pretty, hand sewn lace curtains still hang at the window.

On your way back downstairs, it is a good idea to grab hold of the fitted perimeter dark wood shelving; don't be concerned about it taking your weight, as the shelves are pretty strong. The last thing you want to do is slip, fall and land in a heap against the wall at the bottom!

You should now have arrived safely back in the kitchen area.

Picture taken from dining area, with view of kitchen in far corner.

Honeysuckle Cottage garden
August 2007

This garden provides approximately a quarter acre of land to the property. It has been fenced all the way around with wooden posts and galvanised wire and a thin strand of barbed wire is threaded all the way along at the top, because there are bullocks (young bulls) grazing in the surrounding fields. The driveway is grassed and the majority of the garden has fruit trees, vegetable plots, greenhouses and sheds, with two outbuildings, the outside privy and the washhouse. These plants, the shrubs and trees, are not all placed in strategic positions: they are dotted about the place, here and there, and would play havoc with anyone who likes to act in an organised manner. Paths around the garden are either gravel or inlaid house bricks placed in the ground. The main lawned area is at the back of the property, where the living room and main bedroom overlook the lawn, pond and gazebo in the far left-hand corner.

There are also a number of raised soil beds used for growing different vegetables. These are constructed with a two-foot-high wooden frame, filled with soil and a mixture of compost and nutrients. These raised beds are quick to warm up in the spring than the surrounding ground - promoting quick growth of seedlings - but not so efficient during colder months. In the winter these raised beds may have been used as hot beds, which are constructed in just the same way, but manure is added to promote vigorous growth of seeds, plants and vegetables, during the cold weather. The hot bed, consists of absolutely fresh horse manure with a high content of straw. It is then left to stand for around three days. As it starts to steam, a gallon of water per foot of manure is then added and the pile is left again for around ten days – it is turned regularly with a fork during this time. After ten days, it should have started to ferment well, produce warmth and be ready to be layered with fine compost and soil. A clear cover is sometimes placed over the top on very cold or frosty days, to keep the warmth inside. The raised soil beds at Honeysuckle Cottage are quite old; they may have been used as hot beds in the past, but do not appear to have this type of fermenting content. Also, even though they are all raised from the ground to protect plants from any possible ground frost, no heat is produced or needed because it is mid summer - they are still rich in nutrients because there is produce growing in abundance.

During this tour of the garden, we are going to walk in a kind of semicircle from the garden gate, along the grassed driveway and around the garden perimeter. We will pass a vegetable and fruit growing area and then continue past outbuildings until we reach the pond. We will then guide you to the middle of the back garden and towards the cottage, visiting the gable side where the oil tank is situated and where the washhouse stands, by the adjoining perimeter hedges. Next, we will take you back around the rear of the property, past the old septic tank, finishing back at the main entrance and driveway.

Let's go now and visit the wonderful Honeysuckle Cottage garden.

There has been heavy rain for quite a number of weeks leading up to this moving day and the grassed driveway is uneven, with holes the size of large tyres, so you need to be careful not to trip.

The five-bar wooden gate is quite rotten in places and remains open. To close the gate, you need literally to lift and drag it over the mud as it is only attached with one hinge at the top – it is probably better to leave it open until we can get a replacement.

To the right of the gate, at the boundary fence of wire and wooden posts, an old chicken shed has been placed without a base, straight onto the uneven grass and mud – damp has soaked up and into the wood frame, giving it a chance to go rotten. It looks as if a good wind will blow it down. The shed overlooks open grazing land and there are bullocks in the field. If curiosity gets the better of them, they may approach the fence and stand in one long line, to watch you.

A little further in front of the shed, a raised soil bed is full to the brim with overgrown spring cabbages and broccoli. Here, asparagus has now gone to seed. In a plot around six feet square, five rows of raspberries are fastened to canes and garden wire. They are covered with a home-made, net fruit cage. Right in the middle of this plot is a huge prickly gooseberry bush. To pick this fruit, you may get caught by the barbed wire on the garden boundary fence or prickled by the bush itself, as you try to avoid trampling the raspberry canes. Next to the raspberries is a glass greenhouse, built on a cement base. The greenhouse is filled with tomato plants and two huge grapevines. These vines are rooted outside and have been trained to grow through a hole in the glass. Their branches are fixed inside the greenhouse with garden wire and provide shade for cucumbers, tomatoes and herbs, like delicate fragrant fresh basil and flat leaf parsley. To the left-hand side of the greenhouse, another raised soil bed (around six feet square) holds five rows of strawberry plants. We have now arrived at the old privy wall where blackberries grow up and over its tiled roof. As you continue to walk along a narrow gravelled path towards the edge of the garden a compost heap held together with thick chicken wire is overflowing with waste cuttings. It doesn't have a lid and could do with being moved, as it is only a few feet away from the cottage entrance door. It might be an idea to dig it out and move the whole thing to somewhere out of sight. As you continue to walk past the perimeter trees, a home-made wooden lean-to, covered in blue plastic sheeting, provides shelter for bits and pieces of junk, including a rusty old bike and iron bits and bobs. All this needs to be cleared or it may attract rats (if it hasn't already) when they seek shelter after the harvest in late August and early September. Next to this junk, there are two large plastic dustbins for household waste and a rather strange huge container full of chicken guts and feathers.

All around the perimeter, mature trees and shrubs like blackberry, plum, elder, hawthorn, sycamore, bullace (trees bearing edible wild plums) and apple flourish – with honeysuckle, wild rose and clematis growing here and there through the hedges. The largest tree is the old Bramley apple. We guess it has to be at least as old and as tall as the cottage – it towers a huge forty feet into the air, with some apple-laden branches even higher. This tree shades a bench made out of an old railway sleeper and there is an arched gap in the trees in front of the bench, showing a view of open fields.

As you continue to walk around the perimeter, a small garden shed, ideal for storing a lawn mower and garden tools, stands ten feet away from a lovely summer house with a veranda – a great place for a hobby room. Or you could even sit in there reading, with the doors wide open, taking in another view of the garden, pond and flower-smothered gazebo. However, at this time, large rows of runner beans protrude right in front of the doorway. Three trenches, each two feet by ten feet, have been gouged from the lawn and canes fixed in them. It does look as if there is going to be a feast of a harvest from these plants very shortly, but they do spoil a view of the main garden. It might be an idea to have them elsewhere in future.

Very near to these runner beans, a three-foot-square raised soil bed is filled with carrots; they seem quite small at the moment, but should only need another month or so before lifting. To the side of this soil bed, rhubarb flourishes next to redcurrant and blackcurrant bushes. A very large angelica herb plant stands proud and towers five feet into the air. This herb has many uses: one is to crystallise the two-inch-thick stems for cake decorating, another is to sweeten food – it may have health benefits too. (However, certain parts of this herb can be harmful or poisonous – I recommend adequate research before attempting any of the angelica's possible applications, internal or external.) Did you know it was commonplace to have an angelica plant in Victorian gardens for medicinal purposes and to keep away the plague?

As you ponder that strange thought, let's walk nearly to the centre of the lawn, to a large twenty-foot plum tree and a small ten-foot apple – the plums are Victoria and the red apples are possibly for eating, although they are rather small at the moment, so it's difficult to tell. Just behind these trees and at the far back of the cottage garden, big umbrella-type weeds grow in abundance. The soil here is damp and the clay holds moisture well – these weeds are flourishing not only here, but around the pond as well. However, they do not stop the growth of other plants and trees in between – like a beautiful ten-foot-tall hazelnut tree with twisty branches or another apple tree, bearing very large hybrid cooking apples, and trees rich with black and white bullace ready for picking mid autumn.

If you take a deep breath, you can't miss the invigorating perfumed fragrances from the nearby gazebo, which overlooks the garden pond. For the best view of this, it's a good idea to walk back to the middle of the lawn and take in the full beauty. The gazebo, which protects the pond, is made from four six-foot-high posts and two pieces of garden fencing panel. It is covered in honeysuckle and what looks very much like a Madam Isaac Pereire rose. They are very well established and form three large arches with blossom hanging around the edges. The plants grow over everything and the gazebo is smothered with beautiful cerise pink roses and honeysuckle flowers, as well as purple clematis. Other plants around the pond are reeds, rosemary, flowering purple thyme, apple mint and other small shrubs.

As you turn to look slightly to the left of the pond, you will notice a small path leading from inside the gazebo and back out the other side – here you can see a brick-built barbecue with sweet peas growing up and along its wall. Other shrubs here are more blackcurrant bushes and fragrant lavender. There is one particular plant which stands out; I believe it to be Philadelphus, with fragrant single white flowers and an invigorating and uplifting smell like no other plant in the garden.

As we walk towards the back left-hand side of the cottage (near the old glass-panelled doors leading into the living room) there is a wooden garden work shed. It is a sturdy structure, painted magnolia to match the cottage walls, and it is attached to the house by a wooden fence painted the same colour. This fence has a door leading through to the lane side (gable side) of the house, and across a gravel path to the wash house. As you walk along this gravel path, you pass the oil tank which supplies the central heating and hot water, and a small two-foot-square raised soil bed with tall blossoming blackberries that are attached to a trellis and grow up the side of the cottage gable wall. Next to this, the brick-built wash house is covered in ivy – probably holding the place together – and honeysuckle grows all around the doorway. If you look inside you will notice it houses a plumbed electric washing machine and shelves for tools. At the back of this wash house there is a partitioned area with warming lamps hanging from the ceiling, where the previous owner reared chicks. Little compartments are sectioned off with wood panelling. Here, the chicks would be hatched in an electric incubator and then housed in these sections under the lamps to keep warm until they were large enough to go on the grass outside. There they would live for only a short few weeks until they were large enough to be despatched (a technical word for killing quickly and humanely) and prepared for the freezer or table.

Re-tracing your steps to the main back garden, back along the gravel path and past the work shed and the glass-panelled house doors, something may catch your eye. Near to the left-hand side of the cottage is an extra-large wooden pallet tray with different sized plant pots on top of it and scattered around it. All these pots are disguising a concrete and cast-iron, two-foot-by-ten-foot, septic tank chamber. Well you may think nothing of going to the toilet if you are used to mains drainage, but here things are a little different. It is quite an unusual curiosity to town folk – underneath the concrete lid, a chamber divided into three sections cleanses and purifies waste and then sends it through pipes back into the dykes beside the lane. We first thought this was a late Victorian cast-iron septic tank chamber but later we learned it may have been home-made around fifty years ago.

Moving swiftly back to where we first started our tour of the garden, you pass another vegetable area with three more raised soil beds – fifteen feet by five feet in the shape of the letter H.   A large ten-foot bay tree provides partial shade for flowering sage, mint and parsley growing around its feet. There is lots of different produce growing here, like spinach, parsnips, lettuce, carrots and artichokes.

Finally, back near the cottage's wooden stable-style door, is another glass greenhouse, stacked with seedlings of all kinds and tomato plants – and a large bucket of the fragrant herb, basil, growing in the corner. Yet another apple tree grows over the top of this greenhouse. We think these may be green eating apples of a hybrid variety. A few feet away, are large overgrown shrubs and trees covered with ivy and blocking a panoramic view of fields and the ever-important sunshine.

So, back full circle we are at the cottage door with clematis and honeysuckle gently hanging all the way around its frame.

Honeysuckle Cottage front door.

Cat stuck up a tree
August 2007

We had only been moved in around ten days. The nearest feeling I can liken it to is when you go on holiday to your favourite place but you have taken all your belongings with you.

It was our mutual decision to let our cats, Kitty and Fudge, out of the house. Frank, Maggie and I were exhausted and falling over them every two minutes amongst boxes and belongings, and the cats' presence made life a little more dangerous. So, out they went. It didn't take long for nine-month old Kitty to rush around like a maniac. Fudge (our great big eight-year-old loveable Garfield look-a-like) just took the 'good life' in his stride. He even looked back at us whilst sitting on the gravel path, as if to say, 'Huh, what's all the fuss about? I'm just fine and dandy here, thank you.'

We had no concerns for Fudge; he was really too fat to wander anywhere. I supposed he would find the nearest tree and sit quite comfortably underneath it, whilst watching any possible approaching prey – if he could be bothered to get up again. Yes, Fudge liked the quiet life, with no distractions, unless he could play with it, kill it and eat it – all within a paw's reach. Kitty on the other hand was very young and had spent the first few months of her life locked inside our house in Wakefield. Her toys were our curtains, the arms of our settee and Fudge. We knew we were going to be moving home and thought it was not a good idea to let her out near a busy road. We kept on telling her, 'Not long now, Kitty, we are going to live in a wonderful, wonderful place where there are trees to climb, birds to watch and nowhere for you to come to any harm.' Actually, our one and only thought about the cats that day was to watch out and listen for them meowing and scratching at the cottage door to come back inside again. Although I managed to also worry about whether they would get lost, so we kept peeking through the window but they were fine. We had boxes to unpack – you know the feeling, when no room is sorted out and there are bags and cases of everything everywhere. Even the simplest of implements, like a knife and fork, can take ten minutes to find.

Pretty soon Kitty found the old Bramley apple tree and decided to climb ten feet into the air, ending up high on a branch. The highest thing she had ever climbed before were our stairs – but here Kitty could have as many field mice as she wanted, and run up and down as many trees as she wanted. The stairs were just a practice. Also, in her excitement, why should she ever consider how to get back down again? She didn't. Kitty was far too focussed on the pigeon resting on the top branch - who could of course fly out of the tree with ease. But, this particular chap was far, far more interesting.

In fact, it's strange, isn't it? I mean the process of actually rescuing a cat from a tree. As you reach for them, they start to climb even higher until it is no longer ten feet in the air where you are risking your safety, but fifteen feet and then twenty feet and then higher and higher. Until, before you realise the risks involved, you are forty feet in the air, clinging to the trunk of a huge, rotting insect-infested old tree. All to save a cat from falling, you risk breaking your bones, and the cat scratches the heck out of you to say 'Thanks for helping!' as you reach for her at the end of the very top branch.

That evening, Kitty was stuck, we spent a lot of time arguing about what to do to get her down from the tree. It was just about dark outside and alarm bells were ringing in my head. Let me explain to you briefly what I mean by 'dark'. This is not a city dark where there are street lights. It is not the 'town' or 'village' dark where there is still the odd lamp or house security light to guide you. When the sun goes down here, it's like God himself has turned off the lights and there are blackout curtains all around. If you have no outside lights, the only way to compensate for the light is to trust in your ears and to sense with your feet – not always a good way. Unless you've had plenty of practice, or there's a clear sky with a full moon, there is no chance of seeing anything without a really good torch. So, with no street lights and no lighting outside – AND someone who forgot to buy a torch – we needed to make a decision pretty soon. We were new to all this. We knew there were badgers, owls and foxes about and didn't know if Kitty climbed down and was out all night, whether they might get her and eat her all up by morning. Also, she might not remember her way back to the cottage door and we hadn't fitted the cat flap yet. Oh goodness, life was so complicated!

Meanwhile, Fudge was resting quietly with his fat full stomach in front of the unlit open fire - possibly dreaming of warm winter cosy evenings. Lying there, sprawled out from top to toe, he just about reached to each side of the half-moon woollen rug. Good for Fudge, with his wishful thinking, he had the best idea. But, Frank, Maggie and I had to get our heads together before we could think about relaxing.

We made a unanimous decision to use 'operation go for it' and set up a rescue plan to get Kitty from the tree. She was only the size of a pint of milk and she seemed very scared. The poor little thing had been there since lunchtime and her meows were very croaky and she was trying to eat the bark on the branch. It was the middle of summer and at lunchtime the sun had shone very brightly and the temperature must have been in the mid-seventies. It was now nearly ten o'clock at night and we could just about see the black silhouettes of objects around us. There was one problem with our plan – we had no ladders! Well, we had a four-foot set of step ladders, that's all, so we needed to improvise.

Together, we carried outside our two-foot-by-four-foot chunky pine dining room table, a smaller three-foot-by-two-foot pine table and the four-foot step ladder. We prised each one sideways through the cottage door, being careful not to scratch or mark the wood. On the gravel, under this old forty-foot-high Bramley apple tree, we placed our dining room table. On top of that, we stood the small table. On top of that, we placed the ladder and then we stopped for a moment to wonder at the madness of the approaching scenario. As if it was the be all and end all of our problems, I then rushed back into the house to get a few tea towels and newspapers for underneath each table leg – to protect the surfaces.

Then, whilst kneeling on the dining table, I carefully stretched up to hold the ladder on the top of the second table and Maggie, being stronger than me, held the small table in place on top of the larger table. Frank took a huge deep breath and then slowly climbed to the top of this ridiculous mountain, in the dark, with his knees knocking and making a 'puss, puss' sound, followed by calling 'Here kitty, kitty'. Maggie was crying, I was shaking and Frank was about to break his neck – all in the name of love for a pet cat.

However, after twenty minutes or so, Frank managed to separate Kitty's claws from the branches to bring her down. He had scratch marks all down his arms and on his face and head.

After bringing all the furniture back into the cottage, it was nearly midnight. Maggie had gone to bed, and I was rummaging around in the kitchen amongst boxes, and trying to put one or two things in an old wooden antique larder cupboard that we bought from the Previous, when I found a bottle of ginger wine. It was very welcome that evening, especially after we settled down and saw a big black beetle, followed by its two friends, scurrying across the kitchen floor towards our bare feet.

Strength of ten men
August 2007

Before any changes: This first picture shows the secluded back of Honeysuckle Cottage. Upstairs an old soft wood framed bedroom window. Downstairs, a pair of old antique French doors lead to the main grassed area, a wooden shed painted country cream shaded by tall trees, the over-grown pond, and a honeysuckle/clematis/rose gazebo. Attached, and to the left-hand side of the cottage is the downstairs bathroom. This corner leads to the cottage entrance door, grassed driveway, chicken sheds, and a five bar entrance gate, which brings you onto Longs Lane.

Access to the oil tank and old wash house is through a wooden door in between the cottage and shed – right of the picture. Not shown in this first picture, but more clearly seen in the following, are two greenhouses, the old privy, fruit trees, a wooden summer house, and another small wooden shed:

In August 2007 the garden was brimming with flowers, fruit and vegetables. This was wonderful and we didn't waste any of it. However, it soon dawned on us that we had purchased a renovation project. (A warning to those who buy a house without getting a Homebuyers Survey!) There was a smell of damp inside our cottage, we could put our finger nail through most of the old window frames, we were also concerned that there may be active woodworm upstairs, and some electrical sockets and light switches didn't work. Outside there were a number of old chicken sheds, without floors. We could see where rats had burrowed through the soil to try and get to the previous owners' livestock. There was no assigned driveway, everywhere was mostly grass. Huge waterlogged 18inch campervan tyre marks were potential traps for any regular size vehicle. There were a few half-finished gravel paths around the garden. Junk, like old bicycles, pieces of iron, lumps of cement and general rubbish had been hidden in most of the perimeter hedges. Trees were overgrown near to the entrance of the cottage and made it awkward to reach the main garden. Branches were also within 10 feet of the mains electric supply cable and the cottage roof.

We thought, to begin, and because the weather was mild, we should concentrate on getting the garden organized. Afterall, the privacy and seclusion it created turned this fairly plain dwelling into a romantic countryside cottage. So once upon another ginger-wine-infused evening we wrote a list, the following morning we made a start. We focused on one job at a time. When that one was finished, we crossed it off, and then moved onto the next. With the garden, we worked from September 2007, right through autumn and winter, and into summer 2012. But it's a continuous project because of regular jobs we need to do living in an old place like this.

With the cottage, we worked from spring 2010 through to spring 2013, continually. Every single day that Frank was not working at his job, from first light, until the sun went down, we worked. Each evening, we had trouble staying awake to eat our meal, mornings' were a haze. Frank worked at his job as a counsellor and psychotherapist one half of the week. The other half, he was a cottage renovator. He didn't rest. The only time we took a break was to take Maggie to the bus stop and collect her again after college. That was it. We were driven by the shock of a lifestyle change, worry about lack of finance, coupled with arguments about whether we should turn the place into our home or put it back on the market and cut our losses. But, filled with resolve, determination, and perhaps stupidity, we continued...

Initially, Frank brought out a new Tarzan part of himself called the 'Keeper of Fire' and burned a lot of the old antique and woodwormed furniture that we innocently bought from the Previous. As Frank also knocked down and dismantled various chicken sheds, old hutches, and cleared old junk out of the hedges, they too joined the fire. The work continued: We dug up and chopped down trees that were blocking the cottage entrance door. Then we re-laid old wobbling paving stones. After getting good advice from our local garden centre, we choose a variety of shrubs that would provide colour most of the year through, along with a good ground coverage: less room for weeds and low maintenance. And so it continued...

The flies
August 2007

Never mind about all new and diverse insects you might meet in the countryside, let me tell you about our flies.

These flies are a breed of their own. I suppose if you live in a town or even a village you will be used to the odd fly in your kitchen. It could be a bluebottle buzzing around, a common house fly or one of those tiny little flies which can be most annoying. Whichever you have experienced, the quicker they depart, the better. They can land on clean surfaces and food and before you know it, they have been sick all over them or left their droppings. Very unhygienic.

This is the norm for most flies – unclean behaviour, and spreading germs and disease from wherever they have been. In the city they could have been eating dog poo earlier, and in the countryside they could have been on a cow's bum or maybe even just hatched from the manure in the field. Who knows? But I tell you, the most common thing is that we really want them out of our living quarters and the quicker the better, because one fly can hatch so many more flies within hours. If we don't get the very last fly on a summer evening before we go to sleep, you can guarantee there will be more by morning. Honest!

This may sound like I am a little obsessed or maybe even paranoid. Well, maybe I am now because the type of flies we get here are quite distinct.

We were completely oblivious to the fly experience until we were actually living it (just like everything about our cottage really). Let me give you an example. Most flies here, like the people and the animals, seem to be tougher because they are brought up in the countryside, so they can bear the elements and are quite strong. It can take a fair whack of old the fly swatter to kill them outright.

Yes, you are correct, your eyes do not deceive, this is a picture of our reliable fly swatter.

This was a special gift given to us from the Previous. They said they wouldn't need it any more and left it with us. We thought it a joke. But it has been our number one most used implement in the summer over the years. It takes a swift action, but once you have the technique, watch out any fly who dares to land anywhere near us.

Instructions for killing flies:

Hold the fly swatter with a relaxed arm and shoulder.

Approach the fly quietly from behind.

Slap the swatter onto the offending insect within a millisecond.

Remove any remains with a clean tissue.

The fly swatter needs to be around two feet long and most important is the flexibility of the flapping plastic bit on the end, which is like a wavy piece of plastic mesh. This means that when your arm and then wrist swipe downwards, the ripple effect travels down the handle and to the plastic mesh, making the 'slap' onto the fly very quick – one swift millisecond.

Also, from long experience, we have learned that the gently and quiet approach from behind the fly can catch them by surprise. If you approach them from the front, they nearly always see you and guess what you are about to do. And when you have thirty flies in the kitchen just before you want to put the dinner out on the table, it is a team work affair and you need to get to it quickly otherwise your food goes cold.

I do feel a little let down really by Mother Nature here, because as you know the title of this book is Breakfast on the Patio and we so much would have loved to have our meals there at each and every opportunity. I really cannot describe to you the utter annoyance of sitting down with a sandwich and cup of tea on the patio when flies want to play a game of tig. They don't go away when you try and waft them with your arm. They are nosey little things - I have never known such hardy and persistent beings in all my life.

The special smelling window stickers don't work, nor do the special little boxes you can put in the corners, which are supposed to poison them. We even tried an electric box above the cooker and Frank nearly electrocuted himself, never mind the flies. It's as if they know what to avoid as they pass a vast history of fly wisdom down through their generations.

The best thing around, and the most satisfying to watch (however ugly and unsightly), are the beautiful (my attempt at sarcasm) fly papers hanging in the four corners of each room.

Sticky fly papers hanging from our beams.

They can attract quite a crew. We have spent many an hour sipping ginger wine and watching as each flying object eventually lands on the sticky glue, thus saving the energy in our arms for some renovation work. I mentioned earlier about us killing each and every fly just before we go to bed or just before we sit down to watch TV. This is because the manure flies, the hardy ones, the ones with boots on, make a most irritating buzzing noise if they are stuck to the fly paper or just investigating the kitchen worktop, so they need to die if we are to have any sanity.

Like most things in this cottage, we have learned to respect them. We cannot control the existence of flies, but we can adjust our life around them. So, we bolt the door and shut all the windows – even when it is absolutely boiling hot outside. That way we may get a night's sleep, even if it feels much like we are in some Mediterranean climate. Reassured we are not going to be annoyed by flies that particular evening, we still become a tasty choice for other crawling insects:

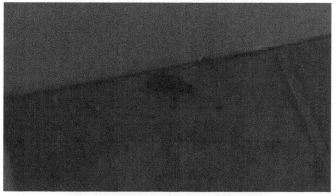

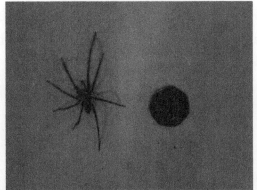

Are we living in a garden shed or am I dreaming?
20th September 2007

I was sitting in bed, kind of semi-upright, with two flat pillows in the small of my back to ease aches and pains and with my shoulders resting on the pine ledge at the head of the bed. I had wrapped around me my home-made cotton sheet cocoon, the ultimate protection to guard against being eaten alive by spiders in the night. If I wrapped this thin cotton sheet loosely around my face, there was less chance of the insects getting through.

Sharing with Frank, I had half of the duvet over me, with a thick blue blanket over that too. I was wearing my last clean item of clothing – well, if you can call it clean as it had not been washed since moving day because we were still not plumbed in for a washer and any launderette was about 20 miles away.

Frank, asleep at the side of me, had the duvet wrapped gently around his face. He had been back at work in Leeds for around two weeks after the planned six-week summer holiday/house move break. He started the work marathon – Monday morning 5.15am he sets off to Leeds, works all day running the school counselling service, stays at his friends over night, works until Wednesday or Thursday lunch, returns home for teatime, only to have a short disrupted sleep and back into our hectic renovation lifestyle. He was breathing heavily and approaching the level of his first sign of a snoring and snorting session. He looked exhausted – his eyes were red-ringed and black – but peaceful. I checked on Maggie earlier, and she also looked peaceful and settled.

Our last caring and sharing thought, just before we fell asleep, was of how to escape this awful madness.

Rescuing Offenders – our learning progression
September 2007

It was part of our Royal Albert Old Country Rose Garden dream to keep hens and ducks – what a fairy-tale idea it was too. Even though we did plenty of research, the books certainly didn't tell us about the actual experience, however informative and factual they may have been. I would certainly suggest to anyone who is considering keeping hens or ducks to take note of what they say, but remember the actual experience will be totally and absolutely different. Our own personal and irresponsible track record was a closely guarded secret, purely through embarrassment at what we had done during our endeavours to settle down as transforming townies. As with other instances, we were just doing our best with the information we had at that time.

I think we must have been exhausted and disorientated when our kind neighbours (I use neighbours very loosely because they live a quarter of a mile away) invited us in for a cup of tea and a viewing of their gardens, or should I say fields, and their small holding too. Our neighbours had lots of cute hens, ducks and turkeys. It was a pleasure to see them all; they looked very healthy and contented, roaming freely about the place. Frank, Maggie and I walked home that night, enthusiastically discussing our plans for which breed of hens and ducks to get once we felt a little more settled. We agreed to put our thoughts away until we grew ideas of how to construct a chicken coop, where it should go, and most of all, how to keep them healthy and happy.

I don't know whether it was shock at moving to a totally different environment to what we were used to or the sheer overwhelming fact that there was so much to do, but Maggie clung to us like there was no tomorrow and we both looked to Frank for direction. However, just a few weeks after moving in, reason seemed to be trampled underfoot by an 'Oh we just can't wait' and 'Let's get some hens today' excited attitude, even though we knew nothing much about them.

The neighbours were encouraging towards us getting hens and recommended we start with rescuing a few from a local farm. This type of hen is locally called an Offender.

The farmers' hens (we are talking about over a hundred here) are all kept together inside a boundary fence and can wander about their field in the daytime. They go into a great big chicken shed to lay their eggs and return to roost at night-time (their eggs are then sold from the farm itself or sent to local shops). When these free-range egg producing machines are around a year old, they are sold on to become an ingredient in pet food or the contents of an odd chicken pie or two. However, sometimes a few get to escape; they clear the fence and go wandering off, probably around the farmyard or towards the jaws of some local fox. These Offenders cannot be put back in with the other hens; it has something to do with health and safety regulations. So they go missing, are sold, given away or despatched.

Naive Frank and I decided to go ahead and rescue a few and keep them in our garden. One afternoon we asked a local farmer if he had any Offenders needing homes and within the hour he turned up at our gate holding six of them upside down by their legs, three in each hand. I remember thinking, as I tilted my head sideways to look down at them, 'They seem strange, so this how you handle hens then, is it?' (Obviously not, but in our naivety etc., etc...) 'Maybe they don't struggle so much like this – they look like they're dead!' The hens were so bedraggled and limp, just hanging there, like they were in some kind of trance. They looked like a reward from poaching, but these ones were alive.

The farmer reached over to hand them to us. I took a hold of their scrawny legs, holding them as delicately as possible, but still at arm's length away, whilst Maggie shivered with teenage repulsion. There we stood, holding these ginger hens in the air, whilst their beady eyes stared back at us – they were probably as dumbfounded as we were about what to do next. We said our thank you to the farmer and walked back into our garden. I was sure I could hear faint distant giggles from the lane as the farmer walked away and wondered if we might now become the new village entertainment. But Frank and I quickly devised a plan to fence them inside a little makeshift circle of chicken wire held up by wooden posts whilst we decided what to do next.

We now had chickens as pets! It was so novel and exciting for us to watch them scratching around, pecking at everything and being very inquisitive.

Before you could say abracadabra, Frank had erected six wooden posts, each four feet tall, with chicken wire fastened around them in a semi-circle and attached to each side of our brand new green and cream plastic, oblong, aesthetically pleasing and cottage matching garden tool box, into which we had put a wooden perch. We even put up a door sign with a picture of a hen at the side of the opening and a drawbridge for them to walk up into their nesting box. Four star accommodation – wonderful!

The new hen coop at the far left of Honeysuckle Cottage garden – Frank's invention.

Frank, get your gun!
October 2007

Within a few months of moving to the countryside and visiting many car boot sales, markets and summer fetes, we had purchased our very first gun.

Where did the idea come from? Well, most of the farmers had one to keep away rats, foxes and so forth from their livestock in the winter. It was another deterrent and quite a norm to living rurally, or so we were told. I am not sure now whether local people were toying with us though. But they said that from harvest time onwards, an air rifle will come in handy when living in the middle of a field. Well, I suppose we probably provided some kind of entertainment for their dull and slower days. I can still imagine folks sitting in their rocking chairs on the porch, with hand over mouth, sniggering at the next eventful incident to occur at Honeysuckle Cottage. So, it doesn't surprise me that people suggested getting a gun; it was maybe all a part of them getting us prepared to live in the 'wild, wild Lincolnshire west'.

But, we learned how to use our .22 calibre air rifle, how to load, aim and fire the thing. We had to get a sight, which is like a barrel-shaped magnifying glass fastened to the top of the rifle. This helps you to get a far better aim on your target. So, I managed to nearly shoot one rat and also shoot a wooden post, only to have the bullet ricochet right back and whoosh past the side of my arm. Ouch!

Also, it is true that when the farmers have finished their harvest around September time, all the animals who were feeding in the fields need to go elsewhere to find food. Our garden, the compost and the chicken pens become a second food source for many a large brown country rat, a slick fox, or a weasel or stoat. They will try and take your livestock when your back is turned and they have no shame; they are hungry.

Frank managed to shoot quite a few rats and then asked me to move their bodies because he found it too upsetting. So I picked up the dead bodies, said a quiet prayer and placed them in the dyke for the owls, hawks, crows or other rats to eat.

I will say, however, it is absolutely not something to boast about. Having a gun requires a huge amount of respect and I would never suggest anyone purchase one without first doing adequate research about how to use it and whether or not a licence is required by law. Even a simple and lightweight rifle like our own needs careful handling and should always be treated with extreme care.

It is also my personal opinion that no wildlife should be shot unless absolutely and totally necessary. We only had to shoot or frighten the odd countryside rat at a choice of wanting to keep our hens. We love Mother Nature's animals, including her rats.

Keeping up the good work
November 2007

After harvesting all the runner beans...

(I apologise for the quality of some of our photographs. In 2007 the camera on my mobile phone was not very good. But I wanted to give the reader a sense of the work we carried out.)

...we removed the raised trenches for these plants from the lawn (in front of summer house) and re-seeded new grass. We also took down two fifteen-foot-by-five-foot raised soil beds, removed the top soil and formed a strawberry patch with an inlaid brick perimeter.

A late harvest.

Getting connected to the outside world
January 2008

It took us six months from moving into Honeysuckle Cottage to get the TV and phone line connected. (The Previous had a TV but it must have been for 'show' because we discovered there wasn't an aerial fitted.) It's amazing what you can find to do when you don't have a square box to sit in front of each morning and evening. To be quite honest, we were overwhelmed with unpacking and getting organised.

We eventually got the telephone company to come along and install a line, when they managed to find us in the wilderness. However, instead of this being a solution to getting connected to the outside world, it just brought more problems. We could hear faint whispers on the line and loud cracking, with intermittent conversations from other people in the village, like, 'Ooooh, yes, Mrs Woodstone', crackle, crackle, 'I can cut your lawn on...' crackle, crackle, 'Ooohh, she never?' crackle, crackle, and 'What did you say vicar?' It was so funny but also annoying because we were having trouble getting a signal for our mobile phones as well as paying for a non-existent land line service. The number of times we would dial a number to be abruptly cut off in mid-conversation was unbelievable and very frustrating to say the least. Poor Ben and John, the telephone engineers, were always here, sitting around our table sharing their woes about life and their lack of internal communications with their employer. 'Well, you know, the bosses won't pay for a new line, we've just got to keep on digging until we find the fault.'

Frank and I looked puzzled because we were supposed to be paying for some kind of service. 'So are you saying we have to pay for a telephone line and listen in to someone else's conversation? Are you saying that is acceptable then?'

'Well, Sheila duck, because of where you live, the telephone cable is buried only two feet down and all along this Longs Lane. Yes, it is antiquated, we know, but the phone company bosses won't pay for something so expensive for just one single property on a lane like this one.'

'So why is the signal so bad?' I returned.

'Its mice, you see, duckie, they like to have a nibble of anything down there in the soil.'

'Do we get a reduction on our phone bill then?' Handing Ben and John another piece of cake.

They both looked at each other and nodded, whatever that was supposed to mean. Then Ben said, 'Let me see what I can do.'

Our bribing with tea and cakes became a habit, especially when we eventually found a local aerial man who came to us and put up a new aerial so we could get a TV signal. It took a couple of attempts to get David to visit and fix up a new system for a fee, but we managed to coax a visit with an offer of home-made cake and calling at his premises to remind him after he didn't turn up the first time – we even drew him a map of how to find us.

Eventually we got our TV, mobile phones with a reasonable signal and a home land line. However, we continued to hear Mrs Woodstone and what a nice lady she is, always baking cakes for the vicar. I do think people should be careful who they gossip about though, as something may be overheard!!

When it came to saving money on our telephone bill, we didn't. It would often take us twenty minutes or so to get through to their customer services and then we had to wait on hold to speak to someone different each time, and explain our whole story over again. We gave up in the end and took up a contract with another company, who probably cost the earth compared to most town folk - they said we had to be charged an extra special fee because our home was rural - but it was helpful to find out what was going on in the world outside our Lincolnshire country cottage.

We didn't see much of Ben and John any more, which was a shame really because I enjoyed our little chats around the dining room table. But I am sure they have plenty of work to keep them busy and there will always be someone else who has a mouse-devoured telephone cable in need of repair.

Ben and John were here!

An earth quake in Lincolnshire
27th February 2008

It was around half past midnight and I was in bed, having fallen asleep with a gardening book. Both bedside lamps were still switched on – I usually leave them lit when Frank is going to be late home. He had been visiting relatives over in Leeds and it was a steady three-hour drive home in the dark. (Our roads can be pretty difficult to drive along when it's dark and there are no street lights, although sometimes, on these single tracks, it can be easier to spot an approaching car's headlights, giving forewarning to slow down.)

I stirred a little as Frank unlocked the house door and tried to creep upstairs, but he managed to find the one step which makes an awful loud creaking sound if you stand on it – this woke me. 'Hello love' Frank whispered.

Sometimes Frank will sit on the edge of our bed to take off his shirt, but this time he had started to undo his buttons on his way up, eager to get into bed and get some rest. He bent down to come through the bedroom doorway and by now I was sitting upright; we both exchanged brief drowsy smiles, followed by 'Journey OK?' and 'Yeah, it was fine, love'.

Then suddenly, from out of nowhere, the house started to move. Oh my – the house was actually trembling! Frank held his hand out to touch the wall and put the other on the wardrobe handle to steady himself. We stared at each other, with eyes wide, as pictures on our walls moved and Jack started barking. We could hear pheasants shouting from the tree tops, calling through the pitch black outside. Then, after about twenty seconds, which seemed like twenty minutes, total silence again. We spent the next few minutes talking about whether the house had subsidence, and then drifted off into a semi-conscious 'more money needed to be spent on our renovation' sleep.

It was the following morning when we put on the TV that we realised our house was not sinking and it was not subsidence – we had experienced an earthquake. In fact the epicentre was in Ludford, near Market Rasen, and it reached a magnitude of around 5.2 and had been felt as far away as the other side of our country, Wales. Fortunately, there was not much damage to our house, perhaps a few loose tiles, that's all. There were however, garden walls, scaffolding and chimney stacks shaken to the ground in Lincolnshire. It happened at a time when few people were out and about, but still caused some casualties.

Fruit cages and compost
February/March 2008

Frank has now constructed two walk-in fruit cages to suit the strawberries and raspberries. This is ideal, because, whilst Frank and I continue to work in the garden, our first attempt at growing fruit and vegetables is evolving in the background. It's something to look forward to.

The old wire framed compost heap was sited about 10 feet away from the cottage door and so we moved it out of sight, to the back of the privy. The contents looked interesting: layers of different types of waste that we knew nothing about eventually became a blackened mass, perfect for adding to traditional compost. It took patience and a long wait to appreciate our compost heap as it slowly fermented each layer turning it into a handful of organic nutrients for the garden. Although, one word of warning: we stopped putting peelings and such on the pile after the farmer's harvest at the end of October. One year, we accumulated a large family of ever developing countryside brown rats in the bottom. They were keeping warm and eating vegetable peel faster than we could shout 'Jack Russsell!)

Jack at Willoughby Woods, near Alford.

Duckies!

April 2008

Feeling rather confident now, we decided how lovely it would be to have a couple of ducks for our pond in the garden. Who wants plastic ones when you can have the real McCoy? We called at a local smallholding where they had some ducklings for sale and went with the owner to the field to choose which little babies to bring home with us. We chose three: two brown ones and one white one. We had no idea what kind they were; they were just ducks to us. But we asked what to feed them and where they should sleep at night, and everything seemed fine.

These cute little things were so very nervous and we were going to just let them loose on our pond. However, I think it was all too much for them and for us too. We spent what seemed like hours chasing them around and trying to find them again when all three disappeared into the four-foot dyke at the side of our cottage. Once we managed to catch them, we put them in a makeshift pen in the middle of the garden with a bowl of water and shelter for a few days – just until they settled down.

A few days later we had a grand ceremony, and announced our garden pond well and truly open for ducks to live long and happily and healthy. Everything was working out really well, until we woke up one morning and the little white one was dead on the lawn. I cried myself to sleep that night. I felt such a failure and so sorry for the poor little thing. The week before, you see, I had had to despatch two of Pecky Sue's offending team because they were very ill. The vet said it would be far cheaper if I could manage to deal with them myself. It just seems the way everyone does things around here but I found it a very difficult thing to do – playing God. Who am I to do this?

'Oh, what are we doing wrong?' I thought to myself.

A few weeks later I started to feel better. The farmer brought us some more Offenders and Frank, Maggie and I enjoyed our garden with our two lovely real-life ducks living on our pond. We called them Justin and Britney, and before we had the conservatory built they would come and peck at the glass-panelled living room doors to be fed. This sounds romantic, doesn't it, and it really is, but the romance soon starts to wear off, just like the paint and all the putty holding the small panes of glass in the frame of the doors, until they start to become loose – and all because we taught our pet ducks it was OK to peck at the glass for a handful of food. Oh dear. So we decided to try our best to ignore them if they came tapping, and did our best to encourage them to stay around the pond, again rewarding them with food for doing so. Soon after, our once lovely pond started to resemble a great big muddy puddle. Well, who'd have thought that two ducks could possibly leave such a trail of destruction behind them? Who'd have thought they could destroy each and every plant, dislodge each and every stone and totally wreck the pond liner within a few weeks? Here we go again! We got our thinking caps on and decided to find a possible solution to bring things back in order.

This was really bad because we were also feeling downhearted at our discoveries in the house, finding woodworm, damp, beetles, etc., etc. So we decided to do the only good thing we could think of. 'Let's set Justin and Britney free,' Frank suggested. 'Yes,' I said, 'what a wonderful idea.'

We decided to take them to a large pond nearby and set them free, let them live the way nature intended. They could have the whole of the pond and fields to play in and be free forever.

We took the cat crate, put them both inside it and walked up our lane. They took to the large pond like ducks to water. From then on, each and every morning I would walk past this pond with our dog Jack, to check they were OK. You could see them splashing around and mingling with the pond weed to find bit and bobs to eat.

We had an almighty row with our friendly neighbours, the ones who invited us in for a cuppa on the day we moved in. They said we were not doing the right thing and that these were domestic ducks, and they would be eaten by the foxes. Oh no! It was early days, and we didn't realise this, we really thought we were setting them free. And what's more, they did seem OK with their new home.

Embarrassed at the ridiculousness of this particular episode, we decided to quickly add another pen to our garden and we dug out a four-foot-by-two-foot pond, and made it around two feet deep. We finished digging the pond, fenced it off with four-foot wire all the way around and went to see if we could find Justin and Britney. Our neighbours were right. We were too late. Our stupidity had left both birds in danger and we found the feathers of one of the poor ducks. However, we did, a few weeks later, manage to rescue Britney and she was fine. We caught her using a huge fishing net whilst sat in a rowing boat that we secretly, cautiously and nervously (neither of us can swim very well) borrowed from the farm and brought her home again.

The Gravel King!
July 2008

Frank ordered a total of 10 tonne of three quarter round gravel from the builders' merchants. It had to be round, the sharp gravel didn't look as comfortable-on-the-eye, and, it didn't settle as well as the round. Gradually, after digging up, flattening and levelling uneven parts of the pathways and drive with a pick, spade, an eight foot 2 x 4 piece of wood and his carpenter's level, he spread the gravel around the place using two small builders' buckets and a rake. The wheel barrow couldn't keep up with the pace, and Frank wouldn't stop-the-job to drive 15 miles up the road to purchase a replacement. (I couldn't believe the strength he found, but our Frank did it!) Underneath the gravel, we tried to use a weed membrane, but it didn't work for us. The gravel kept on sliding about the place, and soon, because of eager digging wild bunny rabbits, the matting grew bald and torn patches appeared everywhere. So we levelled the ground and put the gravel straight on top. Then, each early spring, we use either environmentally friendly weed killers or put the job of weeding on our weekly list of regular jobs-to-do, along with re-filling regular holes that rabbits and badgers dig in the garden. Those are just two of the many little irritating weekly jobs we now have to do. It's part of the cost of living in a location surrounded by fields and open countryside.

Growing paranoia
August 2008

I hear birds singing and chattering, and discussing which delicious fruit breakfast they are going to have this one morning. The pitter patter of rain on the doorstep as Fudge, our cat, sits in the doorway watching the cows chew the lush green grass. The 'click, click' and 'scratch, scratch' of the big black beetles on and under the wooden floorboards. Does all this sound normal to you?

The distant shout of the pheasant who lives in the hedge – calling to its companion. The buzzing and piling up of poo from the flies who were resting gently on my empty breakfast bowl. The buzzing of dying flies trying in vain to escape the oh-so-delightful-to-look-at fly papers – eighteen for the price of two, a supply and demand bargain from our local village hardware store.

We make lists every day, of things to do – oh, how nice it feels to tick something off. But even saying the word 'tick' makes my shoulders jerk – insects, fleas, spiders, flies. Oh help me, it's awful!

There are lots of varieties of insects. My paranoid thoughts wonder if they are available in different flavours and maybe we can eat them, just like they keep on trying to eat us. I even think, maybe we could start a new trend and introduce the delicacy of spiders' legs at the village food market. Would anyone notice? Really? Maybe even with their poo droppings as toppings?

I sit, curled up on our – purchased from the Previous - lovely Victorian antique tapestry two-seater settee, and it's as hard as rock! It feels like something is living in it too because they keep on creeping out of their nest and taking a bite of my flesh!

I am still wearing the same sandals as the day we moved in - I only remove them for bed. Their straps have made a permanent imprint on my feet, where they are fixed in their protective position.

'My wonderful sandals, my neurotic mind sings, 'I love my sandals, my guard and protection against the awesome biting black beetles.'

Did I really rub foot cream into my face last night because my skin has become sore from spending too much time working in the garden? Am I really filing my feet every day because they too have become hardened like sea bashed boulders on a deserted beach?

Is my life turning into some kind of nightmare?

The charity shop
August 2008

I had to get out and socialise, because the isolation here can sometimes be such a contrast to the hustle and bustle of city life. Back in Yorkshire, we didn't live in the middle of a city, but we lived on an estate where no more than five minutes would pass before we saw a human being either drive or walk by our home. We had high street shops a short five minute drive away and the corner shop was, literally, just around our corner – people were everywhere.

Within only a short time of living at Honeysuckle Cottage I found myself starting to talk to the animals. Greeting the bullocks in the field with a hello and telling them what kind of day I was having, started to seem normal to me. On the positive side acknowledging a butterfly and saying out loud how beautiful it looks is not such a bad thing, as it seemed to bring with it a real sense of closeness to nature. We even named regular birds who visited our garden. Percy the pheasant and his lady friend would sit on our fence and shout to be fed each morning at 6 a.m. to coincide with the hens' feeding time. He would feed just a few inches away from me and make a wonderful cooing noise in acceptance of the breakfast I had served him and his lady friend. The wood pigeons fed from my hands and brought their young to learn feeding skills on our garden lawn. The mother swift taught her young to dare and take flight from our garden wire fence. One by one they would take turns at mini flights into the air and back again, until they could spread their wings with confidence. The tiniest bunny rabbits skipped around the garden, too young to be out alone. I watched and talked to them as they nibbled at our newly planted seedlings – not wanting to stop them, because they too share their home here with us. The blackbird runs and skips through the hedges, chuntering, whilst eating pieces of windfall apples. Starting in early spring and lasting most of the year, birds build their nests, providing more life to our surroundings. Bees are busily working all the time the sun shines, passing pollen from flower bud to petal. They don't distinguish which flower looks best; their most important job is to pollinate, again creating even more life. I can hear Borris the badger and his wife sniffing in the hedgerow at dawn and scratching in the soil for insects. Their young cubs play in the field, unaware they are being watched and enjoyed by that quiet lady at Honeysuckle Cottage.

My friend the wood pigeon – taking a break.

But there comes a time when to keep myself from being swallowed up by all this wilderness talk, I should take myself out and meet some people. I couldn't think of a better way than to put something back into the community by helping out at a local charity shop. Also, after 12 months isolation, it was certainly needed – a place to escape from our renovation world and a chance to meet some human beings and share real life. Otherwise, apart from the odd visitor, I would have forgotten about conversation altogether.

Our local charity shop is unlike most, as it is more of a community shop. Foremost, they supply support to local village folk. They have a range of recycled clothes, and kitchen and home items at knock-down prices that are certainly not available in any high street store, and stock goes at a bargain price to the first come, first served customers. They rely on holiday visitors during the summer to keep a good financial turnover and stock is often replenished by generous donations from all manner of people. The first thing local people think about when they clear out their belongings, even those of high status, is to bring their bags to our charity shop.

Another important aspect of our charity shop is the mutual support, chit chat and banter amongst other volunteers and regular local customers. Most people know each other around our countryside because the population is sparse and because it has been their home for generations. It can be difficult to hide and even if you do try, gossip will soon take some form or another.

One thing the manageress of the charity shop said when I first started volunteering was, 'If you don't give 'em any gossip they make it up anyway.' I thought she was joking, but it is true. It astonishes me some of the things I hear. Someone lost a sheep to a fox and it was called sheep rustling and the reported story in the local papers was that all his sheep went missing – it's true, really. And there is a man who dresses like Doctor Who; he really does, honestly. There is also a kind-hearted man who goes around on market day dressed up for charity as a Garden Gnome – but he never changes, he wears the same clothes all year around and everyone thinks this is normal. (Sorry Ron, God Bless you for collecting lots of money for charity over the years.) There is a woman called 'Big Sally' and she looks just like she walked off the set of a country farm TV series with her rosy cheeks, flowered pinny, straw hat and wicker basket. Only the difference with Big Sally is her aggressiveness towards other people. She has been known to slap the odd person who gets in her way, and even the local policeman hides from her. When she enters our shop, we all take a fast intake of breath and pretend to be busy doing something, like folding clothes or rearranging books. Big Sally is deaf and thinks we all are too, so she will bellow her presence, making all the windows rattle. Believe me, she does! This charity shop is a wonderful place to go and escape, even though the nearest thing to health and safety is having a drop of whisky before you arrive.

So, this is what I call socialising; it didn't take me long until I transformed into what folk call 'local'. But we are still remembered as the quiet couple from Yorkshire who bought that old run-down cottage up Longs Lane in the middle of the field – I guess we are getting there though.

At the charity shop I have made lots of new friends. My sanity has now been saved by the Ladies (or recycled teenagers, as they like to be known) whom I would like to thank for the warm welcome into their local world. So far as gossip about me is concerned, goodness knows what they do say. I wish they would wait until I leave the shop before they start. On many occasions, I can hear folk talking about something I may have done last week in my garden or where I get my grocery shopping and how many hens we have and how tired I may have looked today. I take it all in my stride and Frank and I have a good laugh about it later when he gets home from work. Gossip is the food locals use to get by. It's amazing that folk in a village six miles away from us know what we did yesterday, before we tell them ourselves. I sometimes wonder whether we have been followed home and local folk have been standing looking through our cottage window with a camera, note pad and pen – a bit of townie paranoia?

A typical day for charity work

It's Tuesday morning, I need to be at the shop anytime in between 12 p.m. and 12.30 p.m. However, if I am any later than 12 p.m., I am in trouble! (Eeek! Sorry Wendy, here I go again, getting into trouble.) So here I stand in my new mink-brown linen summer casual jacket of a well-known famous label, covering a flimsy, pretty, flowered, feminine button-up blouse and a long flowing lined cotton skirt to match. I have good quality new Italian leather strap sandals and a petite, designer shoulder strap handbag in brown leather. My hair is tied in a neat bun at the back of my head with a ribbon to hold it together. I do not wear make-up because my Ma Larkin cheeks are already rosy from our healthy atmosphere. I have a wicker basket to hold my shopping and am armed with new donations from our cottage – I am ready for action.

Today at the charity shop will be surreal, as always. We will eat home-made cream buns at the till and drink plenty of tea. We will put the world to rights with any available customer and share a laugh, a hug and mutual support with good, kind and caring friends. We will recycle so much from our own wardrobe that we end up wearing each other's clothes.

A word of warning though; customers should be aware they are entering at their own risk and haggle at peril. If anyone offers a price for something other than what the manageress has written on her piece of cardboard in felt tip, they will be promptly chased out with a broom or an old hockey stick. And another thing, there are no signs on the door or shop window of our closing times, but when the charity clock reaches 3 p.m. everyone must leave. We stand at the entrance door with it locked and our fingers tapping impatiently on the keys, whilst motioning everyone to leave because we are about to close. In the countryside you see, needs are a must! Our hens need feeding, Mrs Johnson's dog needs a walk, Elsie needs to bring in her washing and

Gladys really must tell her neighbour Eunice about what David said about Arthur.

Our wonderful chicken zoo!

Chicken zoo
September 2008

Wait for this, our pen was not high enough! Well, we didn't know that hens could jump that high. Did you? These ginger hybrid hens can jump to the top of a four-foot fence and get out. Of course they can, that is how they got out and became Offenders in the first place. Silly me! Not only that, they can rake up flowers, plants and tree roots in minutes in their search for worms or insects. These little dears wanted a different kind of garden to us, we had a real communication problem with them. Time after time we had only been inside for an hour to have our tea and afterwards we entered a garden of disaster. Chasing hens to get them back again was like a fast forward Benny Hill film.

Another time, after popping into the local village for some milk, our garden was not quite the wonderful Eden upon our return. All those lovely arranged primroses, fuchsias and daisies were now flat on the floor like a colourful carpet trodden down by these clucking Offenders. I cannot think of anything worse than trying to have a garden and hens at the same time. It does not work. BELIEVE ME! Unless you erect a pen with six-foot-high wire netting walls those hens are going to get out, even if you clip their wing feathers.

Escapees taking dust baths under our caravan.

But we loved them, all six of them, or however many we were left with, the lovely gingery little hennies who provided us with six eggs a day. That is thirty-six eggs a week. The average family doesn't eat thirty-six eggs a week so we gave quite a lot away, until, on one occasion, I accidentally dropped one on the floor in the pen whilst collecting them from the hens' nesting box, and lo and behold we had six little vacuum cleaners all around, pecking up not only the egg and yolk, but the shell too. I felt sick to my stomach, but apparently this is quite normal too, and it can be a habit they get into. After that episode I was very careful to not drop any eggs just in case it happened again. After all, I didn't want our ladies thinking this is what was expected of them or that it was some kind of game. No, I didn't need to teach them anything because in that one instant they had decided that for themselves – it was now their new job! In fact, I think they probably had a meeting that very evening whilst sitting on their perches and doing their knitting.

'Yeah, Pecky Sue, let's start and eat all our eggs.' In fact, as soon as Pecky Sue pooped out her egg, they all dive-bombed it and ate every last scrap. Again, no more eggies for us. Ok, so this was the end of our egg production line and we now had a race each morning to see who could get to them, us or these lovely ginger-faced vultures.

We had a word with the local farmer who gave them to us and he said, 'Well, if that's what they wanna do, then that's what they wanna do', sniggering as he turned to walk away.

At this time, I think we were still providing refreshing entertainment for the village. Best really to keep our mouths shut and learn as we went along on our own instead of asking silly questions of someone who has been rearing chickens since the day they were born. But, I do know one thing, these hens were a headache, until one day the farmer was passing and said, 'You evor fought abooot getting a cock?' Dumbfounded, we had no idea what he was talking about, but he said it would keep the ladies busy and under control – so that is what we did, but not before we had a ridiculous idea about a hen tunnel as an activity for Pecky Sue and her friends. We were considering digging a tunnel from the back of our garden, through the hedges and into the field so the hens could go into the farmer's field next door in the day and come home at night through the plastic 'Eurotunnel'. We had already spoken to the owner of this field and he was absolutely fine with our hens roaming around with his young bulls and we thought it was a good way for them to have a free-range lifestyle. But what would the neighbours think? Probably that the townies were at it again! Needless to say, we changed our minds.

Septic Sid
November 2008

The old cast iron septic tank was probably the most curious thing we discovered in the garden. This strange looking oblong monstrosity was covered by a very heavy solid concrete and iron lid. On top of that, a home-made crate, housing pretty smelling different plants, like lemon mint and lavender.

We could barely lift the lid together, it was an accident waiting to happen. But for our first venture, we managed to prop it up and then we telephoned Septic Sid (our term of endearment for the septic tank people) to come and empty it. We had no idea what we were doing, Sid kindly explained it all to us: Our waste flows into the first chamber, and slowly-but-surely, it filters through two other gravel chambers and trickles into the last one where it flows freely out through a small pipe as clear fluid into the dyke. We even climbed into the dyke at the nearside Longs Lane to check that this was true, and it was, clear water flowed out, and so long as we used 100% environmentally friendly toilet paper and cleaning fluids, it didn't harm the wildlife. Fantastic. This was quite a learning curve for us, something which would probably be a taboo subject to most people without a septic tank. But, we found it interesting to find out how human waste could be transformed back into nature. After Septic Sid came the first time, unfortunately for Frank, he had to climb inside the chamber and replace the gravel. That was a one-time-only event. We wanted to make sure it worked properly and Septic Sid suggested that we did this and put a wire mesh gauze over the opening to the pipe which filters out into the dyke. This was to prevent any gravel travelling through and blocking in the pipe. Once we cleared the chambers out, hosed the whole thing down, we filled one section with larger size gravel, and smaller pea size gravel in the second, and swiftly put the lid back down. As the lid to was too heavy for us to handle, Frank had an idea. The flat Perspex roofing that is used for house conservatories cut-to-size, could be a perfect light-weight lid for the septic tank. We bought a piece from our local merchant in the darkest colour available - it looked much like very dark sunglasses. Frank made a new wood crate to sit on top of that, and we put on planters with lots of colourful and fragrant flowers. Maybe some of you will wonder about a possible smell? To our surprise too, it didn't. So long as we didn't disturb the contents or lift the lid, we forgot it was there, working perfectly in the background. We put a note on our calendar and had it emptied around every 18 months to 2 years.

Frank dug various gravel soak-a-ways around the garden, to prevent possible standing water from rainy weather. A heavy percentage of clay in the soil made puddles stay around for much longer. So he dug down about two feet, around the septic tank, patio and paving stones. A good fill with sand and gravel made a perfect drain for any downpour.

Working through Christmas
December 2008

Kitty discovered a well behind the pond. The poor cat fell down there. Fortunately for her, we were working in the garden when it happened. Hearing a 'splosh' sound, Frank managed to rescue her straight away. We didn't make a feature of the well, but made it safe by placing a thick wire meshing over the top and made sure it was firmly in place. With the ongoing and constant jobs, we felt it was too much hard work to try and make something of it, so we made it safe instead. Perhaps this is something we could look at in the future. There were so many other jobs calling us, like the old brick built wash house. It was suffocated with ivy growing up the wall and over the entire roof. Frank carefully chopped and clipped it away to reveal that the red tiles were not fixed to anything. After a desperate sigh, Frank decided to leave the ivy to grow back. Especially after discovering a crack through the brickwork. But, this old wash house served its purpose, housing our washer, dryer, spare paint pots, ladders and the scaffolding. Putting a new roof on this old building, or even demolishing it, felt too much for us. We were too tired, and the cottage was calling us. It joined a list of 'things to do in the near future', along with cutting off the faulty electrics.

Sleep!
January 2009

Every night, whilst Frank and I slept in our hats, scarfs and often the clothes we had worked in that day, we knew there was at least one urgent job we had to do. Sometimes, as tiredness and paranoia swam around our aching bodies, we felt like the cottage was calling to us, constantly asking to be repaired or renewed. Unless we closed our eyes, needy yearns were everywhere.

The internal bedroom wall was damp. The single glazed window needed replacing too, but there was no point in doing so until we renewed the broken guttering outside. Frank said that was the culprit. Each time it rained, the water poured down the outside wall and then tracked into the bedroom. Over some time, it had made the internal wall wet through. We had to do something about it pretty soon. We didn't have much money, but if we could replace the guttering ourselves, then the penetrating damp could be drying whilst we continued with the external and gardening jobs, and whilst Frank went out to earn more money to pay for our next potential jobs: new Upvc windows, conservatory and new cottage door.

Our bed soon became a welcome place to rest and sleep (albeit often disturbed by visiting creatures in the night.) We were high on pure nature and, what seemed like, near pure oxygen too. With no pollution or fumes here at all – apart from the odd manure smell – the fresh air eventually helped to induce a deep, deep slumber, each and every evening.

When we first viewed the property, I remember the Previous saying to me, 'You don't mind work then, do you?' I thought nothing of it. 'What are they talking about?' I thought, in my naive way. But we soon came to realise the meaning of their words. Or maybe it is that Frank understood and presumed I did too? Who knows? But one thing I do know, tiredness took on a new meaning in the bedroom department. Any possible loud noises or movements were from deep open-mouthed breaths just before the echo of a snort – and sleep!

In our room the bed slopes downwards by about eight inches towards the window. To stop some of the windy weather from blowing through our single glazed window, we fastened blankets up to the frame during winter, with thick velvet curtains in front of them. However, we still needed to wear woollen hats to keep warm. If we didn't put our hats on, the evening started off well because we were warm enough to fall asleep; however, as the temperature dropped outside in the early hours, the cold seemed to seep through the brickwork and we then woke up absolutely freezing. (We think our experience of the coldness is because we live in an area where there are no other buildings to break up the outside temperature.) I also found it useful to make a long, flat pillow the size of our bed head and fasten it with ribbons to the iron bedposts. This stopped us getting a stiff neck through the night.

Our bedtime hats

We moved our bed around so many times; sleeping on a slope felt really strange at first. We even tried putting large plastic pots and pieces of wood under the bed legs, but that felt a little unnerving as it rocked when we moved around or turned over. So we settled for the bed to be facing east, with the window on the right at Frank's side, and towards the fitted wardrobes and en suite. Every so often, we needed to move the bed back towards the middle of our room again because each evening it would slide a little closer towards the window, although, as yet, Frank has managed not to slip and fall through it.

We would often sleep in our clothes and I only removed my sandals or socks and slippers to get into bed. My feet felt sore with the cold and the draughts from the gaps under each internal door and the open floor boards - we couldn't do everything at once. We really needed to finish getting the garden under control and into some kind of order and poor

Frank had to do the majority of the work. It was the garden that really made and complemented the cottage – it was important to us to clear it up and make it 'in keeping' with a country atmosphere.

When it came to draughts in the bedroom, the old wooden stable-style cottage entrance door was the main culprit – we soon felt the cold upstairs. It blew up through the small gaps in between the floorboards and under the doorways too. So we used two door curtains here. One was made from a cut up synthetic duvet, with a cotton slip over it, and that was inserted into the frame when the door was closed. We also used a long, full-length heavy velvet curtain. Because our cottage was so old, its original wooden doors (and gaps from one inch to one foot at either end) looked so in character that we wanted to keep them, even though it was freezing in the winter. However, one thing I will say, our bodies adjusted somewhat to the colder environment because when we went and visited relatives over in Leeds and Wakefield, we were forever taking off layers of clothes and feeling suffocated by their new-fangled double glazing and gas central heating, whilst choking on their plug-in electrical air fresheners. At home, we didn't want to spoil the atmosphere of our old magical character cottage and our natural environment. And we didn't have the money to buy those plug-in air fresheners in the first place. Money was running out, paying for the renovation materials; we had to prioritise items like fixing the oil fuelled central heating boiler for the winter.

The elusive sparkie
March 2009

Imaginations can run wild here. The noises can quickly feel like our dreams or nightmares are real. Especially if it's pitch black and you need to go out to empty the bin and your torch batteries have run out. Rustles in the hedges, twit twoos in the trees and crunching footsteps on the gravel – could they be rats, mice, owls, pheasants, grass snakes, wood pigeons, foxes, deer, herons, swans, ducks, moths, flies, beetles, paranoia?

'A torch is paramount,' Frank was always going on about his torches. Lined up like toy soldiers, they had their own place on our kitchen window ledge. I thought he was being silly and on some kind of boy's toys collecting binge. But after the cat-stuck-up-the-tree incident, we made sure Duracell were kept in business. Each evening our house was in pure darkness. This was fine by us because we were inside, busy unpacking and dodging beetles. We had other things on our mind. However, it was not very reassuring when it came to the possibility of any intruders or visitors. Remember, our external double living room doors? Still no lock! The small kitchen window? Remove the clips and lift it out! At least if we had light, Billy Burglar could be seen and chased down the bumpy lane with a brush.

So we decided to arrange for a couple of outside security lights to be fitted. Now that decision sounds so simple, doesn't it? It took us three whole months to get an electrician to come to our cottage. We don't know if it was because we were not yet considered as local, the tone of our voice, what we asked for or where we lived, but no one ever turned up. We would wait in all day sometimes, expecting a visit from a friendly face to fix up our lights, but there was no one to be seen anywhere. Surely, what we were asking was not unreasonable? OK, it was only a small job, but a local sparkie would appreciate a little pin money, home-made cake and a chat? Surely?

One day, when we were on our day-trip to get the grocery shopping, there was a sign on a cottage saying something like Local Electric Man. We slammed on the brakes, reversed backwards with urgency and went to knock at his door. At last, we had found someone to bring light to our dark evenings. After a brief chat, we arranged for this Local Electric Man, Sam, to call the following week.

After ringing us on his mobile phone for directions because he got lost on the way, Sam, finally arrived mid-afternoon. As far as the crow flies, he only lived three miles away, but couldn't find our cottage, which we found really surprising. Although, the more we spoke to local people, the more we realised that if folk do not have their own transport, the less likely it is they will know the whereabouts of small villages like ours. Also, if public transport doesn't go through a particular village, then people are less likely to know it actually exists. Maybe all the phone calls we made to different electricians over the past few weeks were successful. Maybe, even now, as I type these words, they are still driving to try and find our cottage. Who knows?

Back to the current job in hand – Sam could hardly get out of his car because he was quite a round man. He asked me to help him get his tool box out of the back of his car, whilst Frank lifted our new ladders out of our shed – Sam had forgotten his own.

Showing us his credentials, he fumbled them back into his pocket and proceeded to rub his chin as he looked at the work that needed to be done to bring light into the garden. 'Mmm, yer need a badger-friendly light, you do, out ere.'

So after a cup of coffee, a few pieces of cake and an hour chatting around the dining room table, he went back home again to fetch more of what he needed. Sam said he would call back around tea time, so we stayed at home and waited – for nothing. He didn't turn up. But we needed to keep hold of this one, as Sam was the only electrician we could get this far, so he wasn't escaping that easily. I gave him a quick telephone call to check to see if everything was OK. He said he was sorry, he needed to feed his hens and would be back tomorrow with the two soda lights for the side of our house.

The next day, we could see Sam's car at the bottom of our lane, chugging along with steam billowing out of the bonnet. Frank and I looked at each other with wonder at the thought of whether we might have to help Sam get back home again, and cringed at the thought of whether his car would make it up our lane.

But he made it alright and we got our lights. These soda lights were a kind of orangey colour; he said this would not deter badgers and they would still come into our garden. Now, unbeknownst to us, it could be that this man had two light fittings he needed to use up (I don't know, maybe they were dusty old ones he had stored in the back of his garage) and he used the excuse of them being special 'badger-friendly' lights. Who knows, we gullible townies would have believed anything at that stage.

Looking back on the day, it was rather like a circus. Sam, bless him, was too big to fit through the loft access to do the wiring, so I had to climb up there and be given instructions. He also wired the on/off switch to the outside of the house, which is really convenient for Billy Burglar. A great big grey switch saying 'on/off': maybe we should just have got a plaque and written on it, 'If you want to burgle our house, just switch off the lights here, come in through the double living room doors or just lift out the kitchen window and help yourself to a paintbrush!'. Oh well, we very quickly sorted this one out and had it put in the correct place.

During more cups of coffee and pieces of cake around the dining room table, Sam told us his life story and we felt so sorry for him because he was recovering from falling from his ladder last week, poor man, so we ended up doing most of the work and clearing his mess away. This was one of our surreal social events in the first year after moving here, and believe me there were lots more. There was one plus though, we made a new human friend.

Four star duck pen
July 2009

As the sun continued to rise, we continued to work: Frank built a duck pen at the front of garden, in view of the double glass-panelled doors. We thought it was a good place because we could sit and watch them splashing about in the two by four feet pond we recently dug out for them. They were a delight to see. Next, Frank went on to construct a larger hen pen alongside the ducks. After around two years though, the duck mess totally ruined the lawn. Between them, the ducks and hens turned the garden into a quagmire. So we moved the pens to the other side of the garden, near to the entrance to the farmers' pasture fields: at the end of our driveway and at either side of the top greenhouse. The farmer said he didn't mind if we wanted to let them into his field. So Frank made a small open-and-close door in the fence. We could let them out when we were home, and bring them back into the pen if we were going away from home. This saved our garden and gave our hens and ducks a healthier free range lifestyle. It also gave the farmer's bullocks something to be more curious about...

Ribbons tied to the top of each wooden post deterred greedy crows.

A bench at the side of our herb patch provided the perfect place to sit.

Chicken zoo 2
August 2009

Bantam hens were cute. Pint sized little lovies! These were half the size of the Offenders, generally purchased privately or on the internet; there are all manner of different types and colours – some are even pure-bred too. But those small hens can be so highly strung (now there's a thought). They can run, hop and skip their way right into the middle of the lettuces and carrots which you have been carefully and lovingly tending to since early spring. Be warned, even cockerels don't tame these flighty things.

We learned a few things about cockerels: You only need one to accompany around six hens, and, he is the boss – there is only one cockerel. So at this stage we had Pecky Sue and her new friends, five cross-bred bantams and one cockerel, called Nelson. We were starting to get a little more confident, giving them all sorts of names like Roger, Mandela, Goth, Houdini, Speckled Jim, Ginger, Pecky Sue and so forth. We were really warming to them and Nelson, our first beautiful cockerel, was the most handsome young chappie around. He looked after his ladies in many ways. But most of all, he stopped them from becoming broody – they didn't have the time – so the remaining rescued, rehabilitated Offenders stopped eating their own eggs. The farmer was correct and it did the trick just wonderfully.

Nelson, with his ladies, Mandela, Ginger and Houdini. In the background, George and Mildred, our Muscovy ducks.

Our latest cockerel, Roger.

Right to left – Moma, Roger, Houdini, Speckled Jim, Goff and Ginger.

We paid £25 for our Nelson (like the one on the packet of Kellogg's Corn Flakes), and the same for his successor Roger (who looked like a pantomime dame with frilly knickers). We also bought three cross-breed bantam hens (to accompany Pecky Sue and her friends) for £25. Quite costly when you consider we buy their feed at £10 a bag and this lasts around eight weeks, straw and wood shavings at £5 each and these last around four months each, and wormer and mite powder twice a year at £10 each. They repay us with possibly an egg each a day. (We once worked this out and if we average the hens laying eggs for around four years and it costing £550 in total per hen, including purchasing the hen itself, building a home-made pen and feeding them, for six eggs a week, they were costing us around £2 a half a dozen. I'm not very good at maths, but overall, it gives you a rough idea. This is a steep price, but we had the reassurance of knowing that whatever goodness we fed them – like the odd bits of grated apple, carrot and broccoli – was going into the eggs and I think they have so much more taste than supermarket ones.) You do also, of course, have the choice of being quite frugal with hens, as long as they are fed a good, balanced diet and have somewhere safe to roost each evening. Somehow, however, it didn't seem to make sense to us though. Instead of making a saving by keeping hens, they actually cost us money. But, until we started to learn from experience, we rescued and kept hens because we loved them and they even had better living accommodation than us.

Not more gardening!
August 2009

As we continued to work around the garden, Frank erected three large fence panels by the left-hand side of the privy. Then, together we then dug out and set in concrete a gatepost six feet tall by one foot in diameter, and fitted a new farm gate.

We decided to paint it green. Why? I don't know: Forest green seemed to blend in better. But the wood was already treated. It didn't really need the paint, and, it didn't stick to the wood either, even though we sanded it down very well. This was one of those small lessons we learned along our journey of home improvements. Every improvement needs to be created with future low maintenance in mind - there's enough for us to do without continually repeating our work. Unfortunately for us, the harsh winter elements put repainting parts of the gate on a yearly basis. It would have been better to have coated it in a dark coloured soak-in stain for smooth wood. In comparison, the rough sawn panels next to the privy were fantastically easy to stain with a soak-in dark green colour. This job was only repeated every 2-3 years. So much easier.

*

Rather than have the lawn strewn with growing vegetables, we decided to separate the two. After moving the hens to the other side of our garden and reseeding the lawn, Frank divided it from the vegetable garden with inlaid house bricks to form an aesthetically pleasing view. It didn't take long for everything to grow back:

In the meantime, Frank also dug out and constructed a ten-foot-by-eight-foot patio with sand, concrete and paving slabs, in front of the summer house, and a small four-foot-by-two-foot paved area for a garden bench near to the large garden pond, and also a one foot down by eighteen feet square for a conservatory, patio and steps. (He planned to get as much preparation complete, including the footings, for our conservatory as he could, before paying a company in to do the complete job.) He had to move a total of 10 tonne of top soil from those patio areas. We continually motivated ourselves with silly thoughts of eating our breakfast on the patio with the birds, bees, hens, pheasants, pigeons, ducks and bunnies. Well, no one could see us, so what did it matter!

We recycled excess soil as rockeries: one near to the cottage door and another at the back and right-hand-side of our garden. Although, one word of warning: Rabbits absolutely love mounds of soil, especially in a quiet and tucked away corner of any garden. Before we knew it, those little blighters had created a warren with loads of little entrances. Our plants were dug up faster than we could re-plant them. Although the bunnies didn't bother the soil by the cottage entrance door, the far corner of the garden, we eventually gave away to Mother nature. But I think it's good, if you have the space, to let some of your garden grow wild. It can be good for birds, bees and other animals that might struggle elsewhere in a man-made environment. The far corners of our cottage garden are a little overgrown, but they grow all manner of pretty wild flowers. We just accept that the bunnies live there now.

Our rockeries.

*

After sanding down and painting the work shed, summer house, small shed and various other outside doors with preserve, we were feeling extremely tired, but pleased with our achievements so far.

Clematis climbing our work shed.

Pond life
August 2009

It was late summer 2009 when we dug out and reformed the fifteen feet by around four feet and two feet wide muddy puddle. There just wasn't a good time to re-do the pond. We knew there were fish, frogs and newts living in there.

Firstly, we put as many of the fish as we could into large buckets of the pond water. Next we started to remove plants and weeds, emptied the water with small buckets, and pulled out the old black sheeting from the floor of the pond. Then we removed any protruding lumps and bumps, and flattened the base as much as possible. A layer of builders' sand made a good leveler for the cut-to-size 25 year guaranteed black pond liner. Once we started to refill the pond, Frank tucked the overlap of the liner underneath the concrete irregular paving stones, where he then cemented them into place. This gave the pond a soft informal view and provided little gaps for cute ditsy flowers and moss to grow inbetween. Again we choose plants that would provide some colour most of the year around. The first thing that anyone noticed in our garden was the pond and the beautiful overhanging clematis and rose gazebo, so we felt it was important to keep this area as vibrant as possible. We also planted various plants such as daisies, foxglove and lilies at the back to enhance the view even more.

*

Summer 2009, we purchased some scaffolding for £100 from a local advert. It had a few patches and dents, but Frank, given his history in the building trade, he thought it safe enough for us to stand on and replace the guttering. He hammered two thick aluminum hooks into the render of the cottage so we could tie the metal frame to it. But this didn't stop minor wobbles. We steadily, and with a few anxious arguments, placed it onto blocks of wood to make the frame level. Next all we needed to do was to keep our nerve as we stood up there. Together we took down the old guttering and replaced it with the best Frank could find, along with a long plastic comb to prevent birds nesting in the eaves. Then, eventually, once we started working inside the cottage, we could go in the roof space (the loft) and remove the old nests. We made sure we did this job in the late summer, to avoid any birds still nesting up there.

Although, much to our surprise, there was a group of sparrows living in the roof space of our downstairs bathroom all year round. We thought that surely they would leave at some time, but that was their home. They returned to sleep there every evening. We could hear them tapping and moving around, like they were having some kind of tea party each evening and guests for breakfast early the next morning. It didn't bother us too much, not like the ones in the upstairs loft space at 4am every day. But, they may have been causing damage to the property for some time, so we had to investigate and remove them. We did this in the kindest possible way: we would sit on the garden bench by the hen pen and count the little sparrows as they left. Each would sit on the edge of the old guttering and fly off somewhere, and return. Once we were sure there was a time when they had all gone out for a few hours, we evicted them, the poor things, and filled any visible spaces with a setting foam. There were plenty more places that these little birds could find to live, like the privy roof opposite or the old Bramley apple tree, so we didn't punish ourselves too much.

*

We needed an office, a space, an escape, away from the cottage and the feel that we needed to work on it all the time. The summer house was an ideal hideaway, as it overlooked the lawn, pond and flowering gazebo. Our internet signal reached the summer house, cuddling up and watching films became a perfect escape. So that we could use this place in the winter, Frank lined out the walls, firstly with polystyrene sheets, placed in between each protruding internal baton, and then Upvc sheeting in a cream wood grain colour. It looked fabulous. It was easy to wipe clean, and much warmer than before. We brought electricity through an underground extension, passed through the same blue tough piping that is used for mains water. Buried two feet under the lawn, this piping was tough enough to withstand all elements of the weather, fully water and nibble proof! It was also easy enough to disconnect if we decided at any time in the future to remove it, because just like an everyday extension, it had an ordinary plug at each end that was passed through a hole in the side of the wall. Just like you may use a plug extension with a circuit breaker whilst using the lawn mower, we had one for the summer house, to be connected or disconnected at any time we needed heat or light in there.

Waggiest tail
August 2009

Jack won First prize for Waggiest Tail and Second Most Handsome Dog at Partney Country Show 2009.

Kitty in the background, kindly counting our fish.

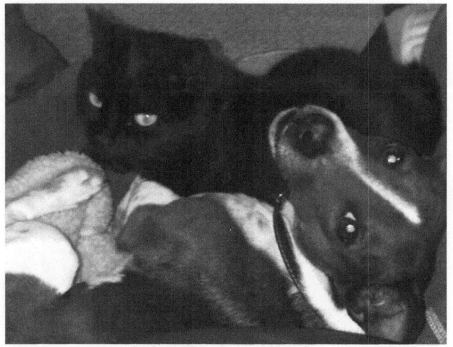

Jack & Kitty, best of friends.

The story of Goth
August 2009

I'd like to tell you something which happened during our infancy of keeping chickens (my hand is over my mouth in disgust and our heads are hung in shame!).

We have a gun, yes? You remember from previous chapters? OK. Mmmm .... Goth, well she was a member of our second batch of hens – the ones we got to accompany Pecky Sue and her friends. She was (God rest her soul) a lovely, but very highly strung mixed black bantam hen with white rings around her eyes. She had a quiff of feathers on her head and looked distinctively like a naughty teenager – though we are not in the habit of culling teenagers.

For us, it was one of those weeks when we had hardly any sleep at all. It was during the summer of 2009, very warm during the evening, but if we opened a window, flies and insects would soon accompany us in our room. We used a fly net up at the window but still the odd buzzing insect managed to lift the netting to get through. I am sure they knew what they were doing, pushing and easing themselves underneath any tiny little gap we may have missed. So our tempers were fraught.

We were still trying to untangle the jungle in parts of our huge garden. Frank kept on reminding me that it was very important, 'outside impressions to other people matter, and, we need to get back control of our garden so we can enjoy living here!' I understood this and slightly agreed, but we only had onlookers from the field in the shape of bullocks. I didn't know that bullocks could gossip! Incidentally, they became so curious at one stage, they pushed part of the fencing down and took themselves for a walk through our flowerbeds. After chewing the kale, lettuce and runner beans, they trampled their way through another fence and made their way onto Longs Lane - but that's a 'head-in-our-hands story for some other time, perhaps when our feelings have numbed a little more.

Our garden was starting to feel like our pride and joy. We worked hard at tackling Mother Nature. But I can't find any plausible excuses for what we are about to tell you...

'That b****y hen's out again!'

'Yes I know, Frank.'

'I thought you were gonna finish making good those holes in the fence to stop rabbits digging.' A naive townie expectation!

'Yes I know, Frank – I have!'

'Then how the heck is that bloomin' hen back in the garden again?'

For three days we watched whilst this clever little madam went out into the field through our home-made gateway, through the hen pen, and then steadily worked her way back into our garden, through her own home-made entrance, whilst our backs were turned. She was a magnificent digging and raking machine and she had steadily rearranged all the rockery plants around our new patio and pond. She pulled up each and every plant, carefully separated the roots from their stems, like getting knots out of long hair with a fine comb, to get to any little insect or worm. We were both livid because no way was this hen ever going to be caught. Goff knew she was being naughty because she had even stopped coming home to roost in her box. That was possibly because we kept trying to catch her with a very large fishing net! She hid in the hedge and slept on a branch somewhere in the outskirts of our garden each night. She waited for first light and then it was a race for us to try and shoo her out of the garden and away from our flowers. One day, she even managed to find our raised soil beds. (We had only just cleared them up after the Bullock episode.) Thinking back, Frank and I cannot believe just how much damage one hen could do to a garden. She dug out our carrot box, pinched lots of strawberries and rearranged the beetroot and lettuce. Something had to be done.

'Right, that's it. Frank, get your gun!'

'What?'

'Get your gun – I can't catch the little so-and-so, we're going to have to shoot it! We can't go on like this. The stupid thing is destroying all our hard work. I've had enough of us arguing about it, go get the gun Frank!'

We sat for about an hour at our patio table, and had just finished drinking a brew of Earl Grey tea from chintzy tea cups and saucers when we had an idea.

Frank agreed he would shoot Goth if I would then rush over and wring her neck immediately to avoid any prolonged pain.

'Oh go on, Sheila, you've done it before. If we work as a team, we can get this thing over with and get on with more important things, like paying the bills!'

'Frank, you're so blasé about it all, do you know what it's like to do that to a hen – obviously not – just shoot it will you!' Then, like some kind of warped western movie, Frank got up from his chair, stretched his arms in the air to crack his knuckles and marched back to the cottage to get our gun. Upon his return, he sat down next to me and rested the air rifle across his lap. He finished off his last drops of tea, slowly wiped a sleeve across his face, and then we both sat there, waiting in silence for Goth to appear. (I am relieved that we had no close neighbours overlooking our strange behaviour!) Frank took aim and I was ready to run and jump on Goth, with my large fishing net. You could hear her moving about in the undergrowth between the shrubs at the back of our garden. But if we got up and approached her, she just ran off again. We needed to sit, watch and wait until she put in an appearance in full view again. So we waited and waited and waited. Until eventually, after several shots, with air rifle pellets all over the floor and a few grazed knees from trying to catch her, we did it. Between us we managed to do the necessary. I took her to the large dyke where the rats, foxes and owls hunt, said a goodbye prayer and left her there to return to Mother Nature.

I walked back home, crying until my eyes were sore. Frank had been crying too, I could tell. He said he hadn't but you could see the red patches at the top of his cheek bones; I recognised the signs. Now we both felt like murderers. We cleared up, went back inside, I did the washing up and Frank took Jack for a walk up the lane.

The following morning, we got up out of bed and drew back our bedroom curtains. Looking out over our beautiful garden we stared, bewildered, at the sight of rockery plants all over the place again. 'What on earth's happening – I thought you put all the hens away last night?'

'I did, love.'

'So, what's this all about then?'

I quickly slipped on my dressing gown and slippers, and dashed downstairs as fast as I could to try and catch the culprit. Who should be at the back door, waiting? Goth!!! She looked as healthy as can be, risen from the dead – and believe me, we did kill her, but there she was right in front of me waiting for her breakfast.

OK, so we thought this bird must deserve a place in our chicken pen so we gave her back her rightful home. We closed the little gate into the field and told her she had to stay inside her pen until she could behave. But, lo and behold, she managed to escape and demolish all over again, so this time we meant business. I quickly and swiftly took the bird and carefully despatched her for good. We just couldn't cope with the disruptions any more.

'There, it's done, Frank,' I said, wiping away more tears.

'OK love, you did your best, come inside now and have a cup of tea.'

The following day, we went out in the car to the village to get some groceries and it was a lovely sunny day. I can remember seeing quite a few local people on our way, chatting and just passing the time of day, very pleasant really – life seemed to be getting back to normal. Well, as normal as it could get considering our ongoing cottage renovation project.

We drove along our lane, stopping to take pictures of butterflies resting in the long grass and then a finch in the hedge and a robin too. Excited to see what they might look like in a photograph and discussing how we could start a scrap book and diary about our adventures here, we soon approached our gateway. But wait, there was something blocking the entrance! Oh my goodness, it was Goth, risen from the dead again! What on earth? The bird was there in front of our car, scratting around the flowerbeds at the side of our gateposts, and she had been raking up the rockery around the postbox. I took a deep breath, turned and looked at Frank, reached for the car door and exhaled very loudly ...

'Right, that's it!' I said in a fury.

I quickly got a hold of the bird and took her into the pen and slammed the field gate closed. 'She's staying,' I shouted back to Frank. 'I can't do this any more.'

Needless to say, after all the pantomime, we did keep Goth and she went on to brood and hatch out a set of fertile eggs. She mothered four chicks and lived a long and healthy life. She didn't get out of the pen again, because we made it six feet high, but she had plenty of room in her ten-foot-by-twenty-foot half-grassed enclosure. We did, however, allow her the occasional day release into the farmer's field, but only whilst we could keep an eye on her and coax her back inside when we were going indoors. I don't know whether she had a little bit of a headache or a stiff neck after our manhandling, maybe even a bullet or two lodged in her throat, but she was certainly a tough cookie.

Goth was one of the last bantam hens we kept before turning to Silkie hens – who incidentally cannot fly, cannot jump very high and, if we let them in the farmer's field to graze, all they want to do is sunbathe under a nearby tree.

This is our favourite, she is a three month old Miniature Bantam
White Silkie Hen and so very tame.

Roads and directions
September 2009

Why is it I am always late for appointments? Well, I really need to put more effort into setting off from home a little more like half an hour too early – this way I may reach my destination. Not that I mind a friendly chat, as there is nothing nicer and more welcome than being accepted into our village. Only last week I had an appointment at the dentist. I set off to go up our lane and saw a neighbour walking her dog. We chatted briefly through the car window about the Muntjac deer that live in the field and the incredible number of hares and rabbits this year. I drove on past the farm and saw another lady in her allotment, we exchanged waves and she urged me to call for tea and cakes. We then had a brief chat about growing tomatoes and peppers and a proposed meeting at the church hall. Before we finished our chat, the farmer was seen approaching in his tractor and I remembered I needed to ask him for a bale of straw for my hens. I got out of the car to go to speak with him about that and end up discussing the waterlogged fields and fish ponds. Oh yes, the dentist – well, I'm afraid I was a little late.

In most cities, if someone stopped their car to speak to me, unless I knew them well, suspicion would fill my mind. But, here, it is just a way of life and most refreshing.

Four years into the lifestyle of country roads we don't really notice them any more; we just accept them and drive along. However, it does take quite a skill and understanding of the wildlife and other drivers. Wood pigeons play 'dare' and almost want you to stop your car before they make a last attempt to fly out of the way. Pheasants walk into your path and then scarper. Then, with a last minute dash, they decide to run back again for a near fatal thud – much like the odd stray chicken too. Night-time is the worst because it can be hard to see a young rabbit and sometimes you don't hear a thing until you look back through your rear view mirror at the ground. Care, consideration and respect need to be applied to the countryside roads, to avoid unnecessary injuries.

From the moment we drive off the motorway and onto the dual carriageway the atmosphere changes; we are nearly in the countryside now. The air is smoother, we can hear birds singing and the pace slows down. Most of those big racing roads disappear into dwindling single tracks – these can seem more like large pathways. These are the roads where only one car can comfortably drive along.

Since moving here, we've learned the unregistered and unspoken politeness code to pull over to the grass verge as much as we can to let another car or vehicle past. Then a friendly wave and smile to each other confirms the exchange of helpfulness. More often than not, two drivers will stop and pass the time of day through their car windows during this exchange. This can take the form of a quick 'thank you' or 'how ya doin'?' to a general chat about who is making cakes for this year's village fete.

Watch out, though, if you don't live here and are out for the day or on holiday and your usual route is the M62 or M25. Or maybe you do live here and know the roads like the 'back of your hand' and so you have maybe started to treat our roads just like the M62 or M25. If you're one of those pushy drivers, the ones who have difficulty in adjusting to our slower pace and who drive at what seems like a yard away from our bumper, trying to push us from the road – take heed and be wise. There have been so many accidents around here. We have trenches and dykes at the side of most roads to allow rainwater to drain off into canals and rivers and eventually the sea. Many a car has ended up sliding into these ditches and some accidents have been quite nasty and people have drowned. I am really not sure why a sheer twenty-foot drop a few inches from your car wheel cannot prompt you to slow down – long and straight roads are obviously too much of a tease to test out a car's speed. I suppose we can't expect someone who lives in a city or with little patience to suddenly change their pace of life when it has taken 'us' nearly two years to adjust into our new lifestyle.

However, maybe this little anecdotal instruction could help.

Here are a few suggestions if you happen to be following a tractor:

Wait until you are within eyesight of the farmer, so he can see you out of his mirror – if he has one.

Don't drive right up his backside, as manure may spill onto your car. He may also slow down if he knows you are urging his vehicle to go faster.

Depending on what kind of day he has had, he may pull over and let you pass. (Farmers are extremely hard working and dedicated people. They work from first light until the dark of night. If their work is not complete, they even work through the evening. This is seven days a week. If there is ever a fine example of achievers, I would vote for farmers any day. They are such a credit to our society.)

Wait until he turns in a different direction to the one you are going. He may even find the next available wide spot in the road and pull over. (You do obviously also have the option to stop your car, do a ten-point turn, avoiding the six feet drops at the side of the road, and find another way to get to your destination.)

Wait until you have a safe place to pass – please though, not on a blind bend like some people do, even if the farmer is only driving at one mile an hour. Meeting another car in the opposite direction could bring your holiday to a prompt end.

Never flash your lights at him; remember some farmers have guns and this journey may take even longer!

When we first moved here, every journey took longer. In fact, the number of times I had to ask directions back to our cottage was embarrassing. It was certainly one way to meet local people – at least I made them laugh. Frank is a little more stubborn than me though and will drive round and round until he eventually reaches his destination. I really can't see the point in running around aimlessly when we could ask a man walking his dog who will probably have more sense about him to know where we are. And, you can guarantee he will appreciate our little chat in the first place; we might even be the only people he has spoken to all day.

There is a little transformation which happens on moving to a rural environment and it can be quite subtle. Road signs are replaced by land marks. By this I don't mean they are physically removed; I mean because we are in a rural environment, there are fewer street and road names. I will never forget the first time we asked for directions to the nearest supermarket. It was much like, 'go up the hill, turn left at the junction, turn right at Teapot Cottage and go straight on to the cow sheds. Now you have a choice to turn left or right, it doesn't matter. Go right along the lane and you'll see some tall trees, turn right and go straight on till you see the ducks in the pond and then you've got a choice. You can either go past the church or along the drain's edge or to the side of Mr White's farm shop.' Amazing! When we go and visit Leeds or Wakefield and people ask directions, they automatically expect the street names. Frank and I now just respond with a blank face, followed by a cheeky smile and wink.

We were once the impatient people who would push and glare at the other driver – we have been there and have worn the tee-shirt many times. We too have been the people on holiday, with no mutual respect for fellow road users, not seeing the one-foot-wide grass verge separating us from a six-foot slip into the water below. We've learned to slow down, enjoy the scenery and drive with a mutual respect. We no longer let fellow 'pushers' intimidate us. Remember, we may know the road better than them. The driver may be on holiday and unable to slow down his pace from a big city or, on the other hand, he may know the road very well and have absolutely no patience whatsoever with us lingerers. Whatever the case, we just – slow down.

Snowy weather in Louth.

Chopping down trees
December 2009

Tall trees are useful around our rural property because they provide protection from the cold wind and rain that would otherwise not be there. In built up areas, the weather is not as noticeable because houses and buildings act as barriers. We had to get a balance between protection and safety.

By late summer 2009, tree growth at the lane side was dangerously near to our cottage roof and touching the electricity supply cables. Fortunately for us, we made a simple telephone call to the electric board and in November 2009 they came along and cut the trees down at Longs Lane side to a more comfortable height of around ten feet. Frank then chopped down the remaining perimeter trees and hedges to the same height, using only a hand saw after the electric one broke. It took us a never-ending eight weeks to chop up, burn and compost three times this amount from the middle of our garden:

Autumn and winter always looks bare and dank in the garden. But when leaves have fallen, it's the best time to trim the hedges and prepare for the new growth the following year.

Unblocking drains
December 2009

Unblocking drains and draining large puddles on Longs Lane became a genuine curiosity. But, it was a full day's job. It took us over a week to get it right and understand how they worked. Our outside drains blocked on two occasions. It didn't take long for us to figure them out. Although standing in the dyke is not a job I would like to revisit anytime soon. Somehow a shower or bath afterwards didn't feel enough to rid being covered in mud from wading about in there. But, thank goodness for drain rods, eh? Each individual wooden rod was fastened together and looked like a chimney sweeps tool but without the brush on the end. We lifted the drain cover by the cottage door, I pushed from this side and Frank stood in the dyke to pull it through there. Then, as we tired and lost our patience with each other, we would swap around and see if either of us could come up with any other bright ideas to free the blockage. In the end, a hose pipe helped to work things free. In future, the best way to prevent this from happening on a regular basis, is to be extremely careful what might slip down the sink. No peelings, fat of any description, no tiny bits and bobs of anything. A small purpose made wire mesh gauze that we bought from our local do-it-yourself merchants was a perfect little gadget to sit in the kitchen sink to stop any little accidents from slipping down and getting stuck. That would save us having to dig up the driveway again to get to the pipes. Although there is something quite therapeutic about freeing a blockage...

Longs Lane is an unmade and un-adopted road. This has its positive side, we get no through traffic because a mile up the road, it is closed off by a farm gate and private property. Harvest time is the busiest, when for around 48 hours solid the farm traffic and combine harvesters are bringing in their harvest.

Frank used our pick to flatten bumps in the lane. Then he dug four or five of these trenches to let excess water drain away from large puddles. This was late January 2009:

Subsequent years, the farmer kindly used his machinery to slice off the embankment at an angle, creating an adverse camber, so that in future water would run off the lane and into the dyke. Thank goodness this was one less job to do.

Mucking out
January 2010

Reluctantly, I tie my hair back, put on my old jogging bottoms, long socks, thermal vest, polo neck, wool jumper, scarf, hat, fleece and Wellington boots. I then collect my rubber gardening gloves from the greenhouse opposite the kitchen door and get a fork, trowel, three large buckets, a rake and a cushion kneeling pad. To clean the food and water dishes, I get a large old washing up bowl and fill it with hot water from the house and place it on the ground outside, near the hen pens. I scrape off any poo or food remnants and put the containers into the hot water to soak. I bring out the mite and louse powder, diatomaceous earth - an organic and natural powder made from single cell algae called diatoms – used on the hens, in their roosting boxes and in their food to deter and kill mites and parasites. (I will then pick up each hen one by one and give them a thorough check for any unusual signs or injuries. I will feel with my hands and look in between their feathers and around their vent area to make sure everything is clean and dry. Then, I sprinkle a little of the diatomaceous earth under their wings and around their vent area.)

I fill bucket one with clean, dry straw bought from the farmer and bucket two with dustless wood shavings bought from the local grain store. I fill the third bucket with warm water infused with a good strong disinfectant and a scrubbing brush.

Next, trying not to slide all over, I get on my hands and knees in very muddy and wet soil. I do my best to get this job over with as soon as is practicably possible. Using the long rake first, I stick it gently to the back of the first of three roosting boxes to move out any mouse or rat or whatever may have crept inside when my back was turned. I do this because there was one occasion I got down on my hands and knees and stuck my head and shoulders in the door to have a large brown rat jump over my shoulder. I cringed at the thought of knowing they can bite. So now I use a long implement first, just to make sure there are no surprises.

Using the rake, I bring all the old straw and wood shavings out of the box and put it on one side to be later placed on the compost or manure pile in the field. I use the fork and trowel to get out any little bits from the corners and then bring over the disinfectant bucket and scrubbing brush. After giving this box a good all-round clean, it usually takes half an hour or so to dry out, and then the surface is ready to be sprinkled with mite and louse powder. I also rub a thin layer on the wooden perch. Next, to begin the layering once more, starting with wood shavings and then a good layer of straw, the cleaning of the hen's roosting boxes is complete.

The last thing I do is check for rat holes in or around the pen; if there are any, I dig them out a little and place broken bricks inside and cover them up again with compacted soil. If I think there is a place which is being used regularly by a rat, I will get the bait box and fill it with poison blocks. Now, don't get me wrong, I love animals and I don't like harming them in any way. However, when they mass produce and start to interfere with our serene garden, for instance, starting to eat the hen food before the hens do and starting to burrow into their bedding, I really do need to take back control. Also, these are not like sewer rats, they are brown country rats and can be around two feet long including their tail, so if they get really hungry they are large enough to try and harm one of our hens. So, I have to also keep a look out and try and deter them by picking up the hens' food regularly and keeping the waste to a minimum.

Earl Grey.

Feeding our hens
January 2010

I fetch the hens' mash feed and mix a measured small amount with water infused with a very small piece of garlic to deter fleas and mites and a couple of drops of apple cider vinegar to encourage good health.

Hens have two stomachs – the first is called a crop, which is rather like a collection pouch at the top of their chest, and the second is called a proventriculus, referred to as their true stomach. When hens eat, food will first fill its crop and will stay there until it softens, before it travels into the proventriculus to be eventually digested through the hen's system. It is important not to over-feed hens with too much of one food at once because the sooner their crop is full, the sooner they will have no room to forage. This can cause an imbalance of their nutrition and we need to keep ours as healthy as possible – leading to fewer visits to the vet and more nutritious eggs for our healthy diet.

I did find it a problem at first, finding a decent and wholesome food for the Silkie hens to eat. They are so small - about the size of a can of pop - their beaks cannot take a usual size chicken feed pellet. After trying different types of feeds we eventually settled with a natural, organic mash which is made by someone in the next village. I also give our hens a mixture of chopped up broccoli heads, grated carrot and grated apple, mixed with a very small amount of corn oil to enable easy digestion. They love this treat, but I only give the fruit and vegetables around once a week. I put a couple of drops of cider vinegar in their water and a small piece of crushed garlic. I usually put their food dish into the pen for twenty minutes in the morning and twenty minutes around mid-afternoon. This is so that nothing else, like the rats and crows, get a chance to eat it - our hens have adapted well to this routine. In between these feeding times, the hens will forage amongst soil and plants for anything instinctively nutritious, like worms, small insects, leaves or grasses.

Despatching
February 2010

If anyone is faced with having to do such a thing, I would suggest that they seek to be taught this task properly, by an experienced professional. I would also suggest that no one attempts to despatch a hen or duck unless absolutely and utterly necessary and they really know the procedure. The animal needs to suffer for the least amount of time possible and to be sent off to its destination in as civilised a manner as possible.

My experience of having to despatch three of Pecky Sue's team (the original Offenders) was because it was something Frank simply would not do. And the farmers' vet suggested it a sensible decision. This was one thing we forgot to discuss before embarking upon hen keeping – who was going to deal with poorly ones? Our hens and ducks were going to be healthy and happy, living the good life and having freedom to roam – once upon a time! In the past we have been used to taking our dog or cat to the vet if they were ill. However, every time your hen has a slight ailment, unless you learn from experience and advice from other hen keepers, it could cost an absolute fortune in vet's fees – especially if you have quite a large stock. So, over the past three years, we have learned from valued lessons. The best up to now is to gather as much past experience and help from other people who already know and understand how to keep chickens healthy, to avoid any illness in the first place. My advice, for what it is worth, is to keep your hens' roosting houses (where they go to lay their eggs and to perch at night) clean and free from any mites or fleas. I also suggest you make sure your hens are wormed regularly to prevent internal problems. It's very important all water and food dishes are cleaned thoroughly and any leftover feed is cleared from the floor. Rats and crows can bring disease into the hen pen, so it's best to deter them. Get used to handling your hens and check around the vent to make sure it is absolutely clean. Also, their droppings should be a nice, solid consistency. If there is anything you are uncertain about, always check with your vet or another experienced person.

Warning: the following is a most unpleasant experience:

It felt like we were playing God, but the farmer has to do this all the time. I can remember when he told us about deathstock after our village parish meeting. He also said, 'Sometimes the vet's not there to help when you need him, you've to get on with it.' I almost didn't want to keep hens any more. But we didn't let the thought of this get in our way even though we were eventually faced with the inevitable. Only this time, it was a total surprise.

There is this one postman – we have various, I think they change shifts regularly – who has been bitten before by a dog during his deliveries and I am always sure to keep our Jack out of his way because he does tend to bark when he senses anyone is frightened. Not that Jack has ever bitten anyone – we brought him up to be gentle and well trained.

However, on this particular day, Frank and I were out weeding in the garden and Jack was sitting by our garden gate, which was open. The postman must have approached our cottage rather slowly because we didn't hear his car this time. Suddenly Jack barked as loud as a giant Alsatian dog, and we dashed from one side of the garden to the other whilst shouting at Jack to stop his noise. During all this commotion, the poor flustered postman handed over our letters and just managed to get through his ordeal. However, one of our hens must have been foraging near the gate. I don't know whether she had been standing on the fence or something, but she appeared to have fallen into the brambles, right at the bottom of the dyke – and she was not moving.

With Frank holding my arm to steady me, I managed to climb down into the dyke and reach through the nettles and sharp brambles. I really don't know how this happened because usually hens just get right out of the way, but when I got hold of her, she didn't struggle. She was breathing fast and her legs were moving, but her head was bent backwards and her neck looked like it was snapped in two. It was obvious to anyone looking that it was well and truly broken and she didn't stand much chance of survival.

Frank and I looked at each other and Frank just said to me, 'OK, do something, quick!'

'THANKS FOR THAT – GREAT, LET ME DO IT, WON'T YOU,' I shouted sarcastically as I cradled the poor thing and took the 'death walk' around to our back garden. Frank said he would come with me for support and encouragement. 'Look love, you've gotta do it, it's gonna die slowly if you don't.'

Now I only have a small body frame and needed a lot of physical strength to do this very quickly. Instinctively, I knelt down on the grass away at the far end of the garden and out of sight from any prying animals, especially our other hens. I put the hen on the ground, gently holding it in between my knees, and carefully laid its neck and head on the grass. Next, I found myself saying a prayer, 'Thank you for everything this hen has offered our world; please take its soul to a better place.' Next, I put one hand gently underneath her head for support and with the other hand I gripped firmly around the correct part of her neck. I quickly gripped tighter, squeezed tighter and twisted upwards at the same time. I held her body tighter in between my knees so she didn't flap too much. Her legs started to jump about a lot and then...I felt the poor thing take her last gasp of air. Tears filled my eyes and I looked up at Frank who was standing above me with his hand over his mouth. 'Oh my God', he said...and he started to cry. I could feel the life of the bird leave as my arms started to let go and its soul seemed to depart from its body, like it was floating away in front of my eyes...I felt so calm. My shoulders started to relax; I closed my eyes and bowed my head. 'Thank you, God, for this precious creature and the joys it brought into our life. Goodbye my darling.' Then I cried.

Our wonderful country cottage

a poem

February 2010

Our sad tired eyes gaze heavily over the view

Of piles of paint pots, dust sheets and brushes

The thought of more work just makes our

Muscles clench –

Join together and run, given the choice

Three years' hard labour

A face of pretence

Garden of Eden, they say

Then why don't they live here instead?

The cottage has eaten our souls

And devoured our life.

We are the cottage

We are work

Sense seems inseparable from madness now

Onwards, upwards and pick up tools

A stiff upper lip – the British Way,

But what about tired and worn?

Lay it to rest?

Sleep another day – sunrise will bring more light

Re-painting and patching render
March 2010 - March 2011

Frank scraped off and repainted the whole cottage by 2011. Firstly we tried a steamer to raise the paint, but it didn't lift very much. We needed to get as much of the old paint off as possible because Frank said, 'I only want to do this once!' I think he wanted to make sure that the new coats of masonry paint would stick well. Also, the paint he was taking off was not of good quality, it had not been prepared properly in the first place and if we were to paint on top of it, the work could be a waste of time. It would start to flake and peel in no time at all. Also, he wanted to treat the base with a mold resistant spray and fill any cracks with a flexible mold resistant filler. Scraping and painting the whole of the outside took all spring 2010 to spring 2011. As the walls were so uneven, he had to improvise with a couple of wallpaper scrapers and trowels. I continued to do the maintenance jobs in the garden, started stripping woodwork in the house and Frank worked like a mad-man using his bare hands and those small tools. In the meantime, we had contractors come along and fit a conservatory and replace the windows and door, but Frank did most of the preparation. With the windows, he removed the old because he wanted to do this delicately. He treated the cottage like a sensitive old lady. Everything he did, he treated her with the upmost respect. Then there was more chance of his work lasting for much longer.

The outside of our old cottage looked wonderful when we finished. It would have been satisfying to have one single job that ended and finished. But, everything required maintaining. Our house took a battering during bad weather, especially after we had the trees cut down to a reachable height. As the house shrunk during cold weather and like something that had been hibernating, stretched during the spring and summer, small cracks appeared in Franks hard work. We accepted that this was just going to be one of those jobs that needed attention at the end of every summer. Again, he would go around with his mold spray, filler and touch-up masonry paint to prepare her walls for another winter. All was well for a few more months, or until the following year.

A light country cream colour brought life back into the old girl. Although our cat didn't mind putting her muddy paw prints on the downstairs bathroom wall as she climbed up and jumped down from the roof to watch the birds. Bird poo was another problem, especially when blackberries were in season! We thought that rain would naturally wash off these marks, but it didn't. Frank wiped it with a cloth and mild soapy water. Very gently does it though, this paint is water based afterall.

Finally, the outside reached the stage where we could have a list of maintenance jobs to do on a regular basis. Those are:

- ✓ Painting/staining sheds/summer house, gates and panels – alternate years.

- ✓ Keeping the pond free from algae – every year, a small string tied pack of barley straw, carefully weighed down with half a brick for around six weeks. This usually does the trick.

- ✓ Clearing up the leaves after the autumn and winter fall – every year.

- ✓ Weeding from April through to late October – a continuous exercise.

- ✓ Filling in holes from badgers, rabbits and other rodents – a continuous exercise.

- ✓ Cleaning out the hen and duck pens – every day.

- ✓ Emptying the water butts – 2-3 times per week.

- ✓ Mowing the lawn – once/twice per week from spring to late autumn.

- ✓ Trimming and pruning shrubs and the perimeter hedging – Once per year.

- ✓ Tending to fruit trees, greenhouse vegetables and hot bed produce – every second day, spring through to late autumn.

✓ We methodically allocated days in the week for outside jobs. Spring, 3-4 days per week, summer, 3-4 days per week, autumn, 1-2 days per week, and winter 1-2 days per week. If we kept up with the jobs this way, we didn't get behind with the maintenance.

Longs lane.

Getting up in the morning
April 2010

The alarm goes off: 'RING RING, RING RING'. It's 5.45 a.m. on 28 April 2010. My hand slaps down quickly to muffle the sound whilst the other feels around to turn on the lamp and find the much needed analgesic and a drink of water. Then, after half an hour of staring at the ceiling and counting all the joins in the wall paper, I feel ready to make a move and get out of bed.

The temperature is cold enough for me to quickly reach for my country cottage clothes, as described below:

- ➢ 1 pair of worn, thick wool long socks, complete with dirt, scuffs and holes.

- ➢ 1 pair of very comfortable (in other words, a size too big) charity shop green canvas trousers, with a belt to hold them up.

- ➢ A paint-splattered green fleece which is a little too short, so not quite long enough to cover my bum, but warm enough to wear for breakfast.

- ➢ Items of underwear to suit.

- ➢ One pair of three-year-old ever faithful sock-stretched and worn-in sandals – ideal as beetle repellent footwear (because the black hooded things just can't seem to climb the heel and sole of these – so they are a safer and more comfortable place for my feet to be.)

I then quietly slide from the side of the bed into my uniform of clothes and head for the stairs, only three feet away from the bedroom door. One hand holds the wall and the other grips a shelf on the way down to prevent a slip on these uneven steps. I remember to take a large stride over the last but one step – the one which is a little loose and makes an eerie haunting creak if you stand on it.

With one hand lifting the kitchen door latch and the other reaching around for another light switch, I bend down, twist and turn to step through the opening and into the kitchen. Now the dog greets me and jumps around like he hasn't had human contact in months and yearns to go outside. Kitty, our cat is scratching at her box. Maybe I should take this opportunity to alleviate any concerns about the cat. Yes, she does have her own box and she is locked away inside it each and every evening. Let me explain why: Kitty is a lovely six-year-old black moggy cat. Like most cats, she is affectionate and enjoys nothing more than to call on her staff when she is cold and wanting a warm lap to sit on. However, there are a few reasons why at 10.30 p.m. each evening she is placed in her pet crate on a feather-filled cushion in a wool-lined bed, complete with hanging water container and a few tasty cat biscuits for supper, and locked inside. She has plenty of room to turn around, stand up and move about because it is very large pet carrier. If we didn't put her in there, cats will be cats and she will bring little presents into the house through the cat flap. Usually baby rats, bunny rabbits, mice and moles; not so many birds, but one or two. Oh, and (I make no apologies for the pictures you may now conjure inside you head – this is the real thing!) the odd headless baby bunny – she eats the head before entering the house and will try and bring the remainder into the kitchen. Maybe she knows the whole body will not go through the cat flap or maybe it's nicer to eat al fresco. Oh, the joys of country living! Blood does clear up quite well from the brick sett floor; it's a little more difficult from the wooden floorboards. So I just have to draw the line because of the number of times when I have climbed downstairs barefoot with work clothes and beetle sandals in arms to feel the squelching of a carcass between my toes!

Another reason we keep her inside overnight is because of the animals outside. During the winter, badgers and foxes and rats do get very hungry. You see, although they are lovely to watch in our garden, when Mother Nature deprives them of enough food, cat is not so bad. So we try to look after our Kitty.

Each morning, Jack, our five-year-old Jack Russell dog, slides out from beneath his sewn-together human person's sleeping bag, which is placed carefully upon a base lined with two-inch foam and covered with a blanket. All fit neatly into a green Labrador-sized, plastic high-side hugging bed. During the daytime, the cat and dog sleep together, the less said about that the better!

I draw back the green velvet door curtain which covers the double wooden stable-style cottage door, lift out the duvet hanging there and open the door to let them both outside. I do all this extremely quietly (rather like tiptoeing on eggshells) because I don't want to wake Earl Grey, our last-years-hatched-out cockerel, who is about thirty feet away in his nesting box and pen with his brothers and sisters. He will 'cock-a-doodle-doo' again and again till he wakes up Frank if I am not careful. So, I slowly undo the half-inch-diameter shootbolt lock and unlock the main lock. Then another shootbolt half way down and one at the bottom – with that one I need to put my foot hard on the bottom of the door to get it open because the rain has made the wood swell. I then unlock another one and carefully open the door to send Jack out. 'Phew, Earl didn't hear us this time.' I close the door, put the kettle on for a cuppa, switch the heating on and start up my computer to write for an hour before Frank wakes up.

For the sake of comparison, to give you an idea: back in Wakefield, Yorkshire, the alarm rings. I can see it because the light from the street lamp shines through the gaps in our bedroom curtains. I reach over to switch it off and can simultaneously hear the heating 'click on' providing a warm gentle heat around the house. I pull back the covers and step into my fur-lined slippers and reach for my dressing gown.

Taking a sip of water from the glass on my bedside cabinet, I take the book I am reading downstairs with me and Kitty greets me in the hope of some breakfast. I cuddle Jack with a morning welcome and feed the cat in the kitchen. I have a good stretch, reach for a croissant I remembered was left from yesterday in the bread bin and pour a drink of fresh orange juice. With a long stretch and deep breath, I slump down onto the velour bucket-style sofa, curl my legs up at the side of me and switch on the TV.

The work shed.

Ah visitors, can we keep them?
May 2010

Overall, not seeing any one day in and day out can lead to quite strange behaviour. I mean, we were working from first light, squeezing every minute out of the day before absolute darkness forced us to go inside to collapse. (Consequently, this led to me having one or two emergency hospital visits and overnight stays.) This ridiculousness carried on for at least the first three years, until my health forced me to slow down. Although, what I find amazing is that our bodies did eventually seem to get used to doing work in a certain way and we could work day in and day out, as if we were almost set on automatic pilot. It was rather like the experiment with Pavlov's dog when he kept feeding it to make it behave in a certain way, and then, even after he stopped rewarding the dog, it still salivated as a reaction to any reminder of the initial task. In our case, we just had to look around our home and then we would think, feel, smell, taste and see work. I don't know about automatic pilot, I think our bodies and minds could have been in shock and disarray for the first few years, maybe longer.

That is why we always welcomed (and still do) our valued visitors. They were (and still are) a wonderful excuse to down tools and stop a job. These people were regarded as a reward for our endeavours.

Here is a list of the visitors we have made cups of tea for and served slices of cake to over the past three years:

There was the shy couple with their two young children who kindly delivered the caravan we purchased from them. They towed it with their car for fifteen miles and then all the way along our muddy and uneven lane. We then all sat around our pine dining table, chatting, drinking tea, and eating my home-made ginger cake (recipe at the back of this book). But here we were, trying to exchange pleasantries with about fifty flying monstrosities trying to lay poo on our cake. Yuuuccckk!

We bought this friendly family's two-berth caravan in the hope that our family and friends in Yorkshire would come over to visit. We thought, if they didn't want to sleep in it, then we would swap our beds and they could have the house – sorted. I conjured romantic scenes of us playing at host and hostess, taking our visitors for local walks and talking to them about all the work we had carried out on our cottage so far. However, let me screech you to a sharp halt just there. The nearest we got to using the caravan was for storage. It started with our vacuum cleaner, then the clothes airer, then one or two bits and bobs, and so on. Now, every so often I dare to unlock the door and have a little sort out for charity, car boot sales and the tip. But it has been serving a different purpose than we first thought. I could laugh so cynically now and roll around on the floor giggling hysterically at the thought of having family or friends visiting, because for all these past few years we have been otherwise obsessively engaged with fulfilling our duties as renovators.

Next there was the antique man and his son from Horncastle. We bought our second-hand leather chesterfield three-seater settee from their shop and they offered to bring it in their van, all the way to our cottage over twenty miles away. They were nice people, and there was nothing to be suspicious or cynical about – they just kindly made the offer. So they followed us home and together we arranged things in the living room and settled down for the afternoon. The man and his son left after tea, and we'd had a really nice time chatting together. One of the casters was missing from the settee and he said if we call in sometime he will keep it on one side. That was over two years ago: we forgot! Been a little busy and there is still a row of Argos catalogues propping up the back of our settee.

A polite couple from our village visited us one evening after dinner, for tea and biscuits, and I really don't know what they made of us. We were only half unpacked, and the sleepless nights were telling when I made them tea after they had asked for coffee. I put sugar and milk in the cups when they had asked for none. Frank and I kept catching each other's glance to indicate a suggestion it was getting late, but to no avail. However, as I sat on the edge of the settee with a side view of our kitchen and dining room, my dull senses soon flinched when two large black beetles scurried across the floor as if there was something exciting going on in the understairs pantry. I felt tension as I tried to check out whether the couple had noticed them too. Somehow, though, they seemed quite relaxed about our informal atmosphere and I am not sure whether two black hooded insects would be the top of their concerns.

Another time, we invited a total stranger into our house to explain to us how our clock worked. We had bought a wonderful postmaster's clock with a relaxing and slow tick, driven by the weighted pendulum. But we just couldn't get it to work. After a little fidgeting and insistence on his part, the man went and broke it! Well, he didn't stay very long after that episode.

Who else was there? Oh yes, our old friends, the ones we fell out with. They stayed a couple of times. We had two lovely weekends sharing the real world with them – but it was not to last. Whether it was because the country air had turned us into some kind of overtired animals or whether it was just that we didn't want to accept our 'then' feelings of having made a huge mistake in moving into the middle of a field, I really don't know, but it wasn't long before both men were about to have a fight in the garden – I'm sure it was only something to do with the remote control for the TV! Can you believe it? There was no alcohol involved and Frank is not an angry man – he was just very, very, very tired.

So, over the past few years, apart from a couple of visits from Mum and Dad, we have had a handful of visitors from our old life. And we can do without them really because sometimes they just remind us of the simple life we once knew before all this madness started in the countryside.

So presently, are we settled down in our warmish cottage, with friends? Well, we haven't any, so that's another thing to tick off our lists.

Pre-renovation house work
June 2010

Pre-renovation: Follow me into the realms of a compulsive obsessive's novice way of rural cleaning – a mud-cleaning and fusty-odour-dispelling experience...

Housework here is very different to a modern home because if it is windy outside any time after completing the cleaning, you can be sure every ounce of dust and mud you just cleared up is going to settle back down on top of our fireplace, tables, settees, floors, and so on. I have to say to myself, 'I've done it, I know I have – even if no one else knows it has been cleaned because it looks just in the same state as when I first started the blooming job.' But I reassure myself, 'Yes, Sheila, it was not a dream, you did clean up an hour ago.' Other priorities are calling so I deem this one finished – even though Frank will come home from work and ask me when I am going to dust the cottage.

The dust from a small area of the kitchen near the external entrance door.

So what do I do? I shake all the dust from the lace doilies and red velvet tablecloth from the pine coffee tables. I take the long feather duster and remove all overnight cobwebs, (I say overnight because this type of dusting needs to be done every day – spiders get busy through the night!) from the ceiling beams in the living room, kitchen and dining room - remembering to dust behind the pictures on the wall, because that is where the spiders hide. Again new webs will appear the very next day, but at least I know I have done them today. Oh, talking about insects, I also pick up dry dead beetles from the wooden floorboards. They are daft, you know; they travel out of whatever crevice they care to live in and then somehow manage to tip themselves onto their backs and die with their legs in the air. Well, at least, most of them die in this position, before they bite. Because when they do bite, they don't let go and you have to pick them off – ouch! Fortunately, they can't climb the stairs, so this crew stay on the ground floor where they have dug a small tunnel underneath the kitchen sink cupboards or in between the gaps on the brick floor to get into our cottage.

Our kitchen sink cupboard.

I take a moment to glance at our windows and their frames, then, whilst exhaling a huge sigh, I swiftly look away – they look so dirty after that thunder storm. I only washed them last week. I just get on with cleaning the living room.

Next I move the furniture and vacuum the floor. Our vacuum cleaner is around ten years old and on its last legs, so if it's not in the mood to work properly, I get a scrubbing brush and a plastic shovel, which can be good for getting any dog and cat hairs up from the rugs. Just one thing: when I'm on my hands and knees vacuuming with the hose I always make sure I get up any mouse droppings, and if there are any, I have a good smell around the back of furniture, in case I need to set a trap or shut Kitty in there for a short while. It is always a good idea to check right under the fire and underneath the sofa because those are the places where neighbours, sitting in the old rocking chair opposite when visiting for tea and biscuits, might see the bit and bobs I have missed. Often I have spotted the odd struggling upside-down beetle shaking its legs – and I am talking about inch long beetles here, not a pretty sight, especially when we are sitting opposite our guest, Mrs Woodstone, who is delicately sipping tea out of a cup and saucer and we are praying the beetle near her foot is not going to find its way onto her shoe and up her stockinged leg. Frank and I try to make polite conversation, whilst gently nudging each other and secretly urging the beetle to die quietly. These little social visits are all we have to hold onto so the last thing we want is for Mrs Woodstone to run down the lane screaming, with her arms in the air, and never come back because we have uninvited guests of the four- and six-legged kind crawling about the place.

A beetle sticking his legs in the air.

Next I take the woollen throw and the fur throw from our settee to give them a good shake outside to rid of all the blobs of mud. I wash all the exposed floorboards with a damp rag and then dry them. We found this a good way to stop the dust from flying about and landing again. All the dust in our house reminds me of when someone has been rubbing down paintwork with sandpaper and somehow it manages to reach each and every available surface. You know what I mean? Well, Honeysuckle Cottage is much like that every few days.

Then I light a natural essential oil candle or burner and put it on the living room table and I spray all the room with a solution of geranium and citronella mixed with water. This seems to get rid of any strong smells from carpets and mats in our downstairs rooms. I also spray each of our ten scatter cushions on the settee. They are clean. It's just I can't seem to get rid of that old musty antique smell which goes with the cottage. I suppose this is one of the quaint countryside cottage fragrances we fell in love with in 2007, but there we go – we need to 'own' our decision, and we made our bed as the saying goes. So, these little fresh smelling natural ingredients help to remove some of this odour, which I am sure we will become accustomed to in the future – not just now though, I haven't quite reached the accepting phase of these wholesome countryside cottage smells.

Next, it's through to the downstairs bathroom. I take the vacuum and use the hose to suck up all the dust from the bathroom floor tiles, being a little careful though because some of the holes in the floor are better full of dust – it keeps out some of the little black hooded blighters, you see. In the bathroom I wipe around the toilet and clean the cast iron bath with a mixture of eucalyptus and tea tree and a few drops of vinegar or lemon juice. I am always careful which cleaning solutions I use. They need to be natural ones because all our fluid is going straight into the outside drains, the septic tank and dykes. The wildlife will be harmed if we use any chemicals.

Whilst on my hands and knees again with the vacuum hose, I am careful not to suck up any complimentary and unrequested presents from our wonderful Kitty. I fetch some kitchen roll, seal the offending article in a plastic bag and put it straight into the dustbin. The remaining blood stains on the floor are then easily removed with a little water infused with vinegar or lemon with tea tree oil.

Next I get out the mop and bucket and fill it with hot water and smelly environmentally friendly disinfectant. I detest using a mop and bucket – I preferred to use a cloth with a bowl and to get on my hands and knees and wipe the dirt up properly. It can take nearly half an hour to wash the kitchen floor properly on my hands and knees compared to five minutes with a mop and bucket. The problem is though, I can still see those streaks in the floor when they dry and it never seems properly clean to me. And besides, if the wind blows tonight it will need doing again tomorrow. But I ain't gonna to do it till next week because, yes, I do have a life outside of this kitchen, honest!

We have three straw mats on the floor of the kitchen area – most of the time during the winter they are really quite muddy, especially the one nearest the door. Well, what can we expect, our lane is an unmade mud road and it continues through to our cottage. So, with help from Frank, I pick up each rug in turn and take it outside and beat it with a large implement. Clouds of dust fill the air and our lungs too. This is quite a physical job and I find it really hard work. Sometimes, it is helpful to hang the rug over the washing line and beat it with a brush or something to get rid of the dust and muck. I do wonder whether we should wear a mask or something when we're doing this job because the amount of dust we cough up at night is amazing.

To finish downstairs, I again wipe all the worktops and shelves to get rid of any surplus dust. During the summer months, fly spots of poo are prevalent and they are everywhere so I need to give everything, especially in the kitchen, a really good wipe. One very important thing to add: never ever leave any food uncovered in the kitchen or something will most definitely find a way in and make a home there. This we learned very quickly from experience – yuck!

Next it is upstairs and into the attic bedroom. Again using the duster I make sure I get as many cobwebs as possible. What I find is that the cracks in the ceiling and walls have loose little bits and they drop to the floor, and this is why I always use the feather duster before cleaning the floorboards, taking care to dodge any small pieces of falling masonry.

I take the vacuum and go around the edges and carefully along the floorboards – again making sure not to get up all the compacted fluff and dust as I really don't want to make a huge opening to invite more spiders and beetles to party inside our home.

Just as an aside, our windows need to be opened each and every day. Upstairs, both bedroom windows are always open on a latch. This is because, being an old house, it needs to breathe. If it doesn't, condensation can build up everywhere and this can invite damp. So that is something we are getting used to, although it is a little draughty when it is cold and minus something degrees outside.

The next and final job is the bedroom and the shower room upstairs. I clean the shower tiles as you would expect and then the shower and the sink. However, the toilet needs a little more attention. We can't put toilet paper down it because it will not flush away. Also, because the water is so hard around here, we have awful limescale marks in the toilet pot. So I scrub it with a solution of vinegar, lemon and bicarbonate of soda and then an environmentally friendly toilet cleaner. We are not sure if there is a leak somewhere because if we don't clean the toilet every day it smells of urine! Oh, and we can only flush it once a day because otherwise we hear the toilet dripping all night long (possibly due to the leak) and when you are trying to sleep in a very quiet cottage, a pin will make a loud noise when it drops, so the sound of water dripping is like torture. That is something else to go on our fixing list.

So, I have stripped the cast iron bed and shaken the feather duvets. We need two duck feather and down duvets, a bedspread and a blanket to keep us warm. We also have a woollen hat each and a pair of thick brushed cotton pyjamas apiece – the less said about that the better. I give everywhere a good wipe and then do the worst job in the world. Frank and I lift the bed and remove four large rugs from underneath the legs and take them downstairs and outside to beat out the dust. The dust is amazing, after only one week.

When I complain about all the dust, Frank says when we get around to renovating the cottage itself, we could just have carpets instead. But that would cover all the beautiful exposed floorboards, which are wide and original, with a rich deep brown colour and a worn look. Also, if we use rugs, the sloping floor is more apparent and this is so in character with the old place.

With a damp rag I wipe away dust from everywhere – the bed head, the pine bedside cabinets, the window sill and picture frames. I then proceed to clean the floor by hand, because using a mop just moves the dust around the place. I get down on the floor and lie stretched out on my tummy and slide carefully under the bed, armed with a damp rag and bowl of warm water. I can only move along and side to side. If I raise my head it bumps on the bed springs above and my hair gets caught up, which can hurt when I can't turn around to try and release it. I hope and pray any spiders that have set up home under there are not going to land on my face – I take deep breaths until the job is over. I can get away with using a mop once a month to clean under the bed, but with all the dust, it is difficult to keep the place really clean and free from muck unless I clean it by hand. All the wiping and wringing the rag out gives me bruises on my elbows, but they do eventually disappear, at least until the wind outside blows once more spreading more dust around our wonderful Honeysuckle Cottage – then it's time to start over again.

I was talking to a lady I volunteer with at a charity shop and we were discussing what it is like to live the countryside. She asked me if I had any regrets. 'No,' I said, 'I love it and would not have anything any different – living so close to nature.' She moved near to Skegness in 1966, the year I was born, and she was at secondary school then. One thing she said and I agree with very much is that if you live in the countryside you have to accept that it is so very different to city life. You have to accept the flies, the spiders, the smells, the mud, etc. By doing that you can live your life. We are getting there slowly.

Living in the cottage whilst it looked like this was a huge
challenge.

Going inside – making a start
July 2010

For three whole years, Honeysuckle cottage was a place to eat and sleep. Instead of unpacking everything, black bin liners and boxes were shoved underneath beds, at the bottom of wardrobes and inside the caravan. Although I do admit to feeling obsessed about insects and flies getting into our belongings. I supposed this is what happens when someone gets overtired whilst they are going through a city to countryside transition. It seemed that we had to learn to share, no matter what we did. If we were going to live in the middle of a field, there was always going to be a bit of compromising to be done with flies and insects in our home. But we did manage to temporary fill most gaps in the beautifully aged wooden floorboards with toilet tissue and newspaper. Only half inch gaps, but that was enough for something, like a spider or beetle, to make a home there. We were damned if we did and damned if we didn't. Collections of dust provided a safe haven for spiders, but if we cleaned up, there was probably a small crevice that would make an ideal dwelling place for something that preferred our warm home to a windy evening outside. Also, I am sure that flies in the countryside are intelligent. Until we replaced the old wooden windows, we cut up pieces of netting and pressed drawing pins into the frame so they could be left open on the latch and let in some fresh air. Then, at least we could breathe on a summers evening. But if the netting wasn't stretched taught enough, one fly would hold it open and wave his friends inside. We couldn't win!

I love animals and nature, but it reached the point where we had to use flea powder and insect killer sprays in the cottage to get some kind of sleep. Each time it was cold or raining outside, loads of spiders and beetles would take refuge. As time moved on, they could even get through the air vents in our Upvc windows! They unpitched their little tents, packed up their awnings and deck chairs, and tootled into our home. On more than one occasion, when I left the door open to go and empty the rubbish, we had two field mice run into the kitchen. It would be different if they contributed towards our huge mortgage.

*

We had to stagger the work in the cottage according to Frank's motivation levels and our current bank balance. Frank was losing his will to continue with any of the jobs. I had had several more visits to hospital because the stress and work was far too much for me. I did my best, but the sleepless nights and worry about money took its toll. I am not very good at accepting my physical limitations and I only wanted to help frank as much as I could. But with that mind set, it soon took me to the nearest A&E department.

But, we continued...

Creativity was our middle name. Initially, we made our own covers for the bathroom and ensuite extractor fans. Plastic bags with large elastic bands. This reduced the nighttime coldness and the dust after a windy day.

Again, we were in the habit of making lists, we needed to prioritise. We had to manage Franks working hours and any contracted work (which couldn't be refused), getting Maggie to and from college (and when she left college, getting her to work), keeping up with routine jobs, like general garden maintenance, and making a start inside the cottage. Already, for over three years, we had worked and worked and worked, just about every single day. But we were desperately trying to make our lives more comfortable by making our living environment more habitable. Hanging thick velvet curtains that were lined with blankets was ridiculous. Halting the washing of clothes because our water pipes had frozen outside. Making the evening meal on a two ring portable gas stove because of electric power cuts. We may as well have been camping.

*

Firstly, we evicted all the spiders and beetles. Then, using a filler and a dark brown flexible sealant, we blocked every single crack, hole or crevice that we could find. In between every single old floorboard, we sealed, properly. The fine gaps at the bottom of skirting, we sealed. Frank had to re-fit much of the skirting board, because it was loose. But as soon as he did this, we sealed it.

In the bathroom, under the bath and in corners, we used expanding spray foam. This worked really well because the Previous hadn't finished the cement and plastering around the drainage pipes. Daylight shone through. We even bought little gauze plug hole covers to stop anything from climbing into the sinks, shower and bath.

*

Honeysuckle Cottage had a damp proof course injected around its perimeter in the late 1990s and that was guaranteed for twenty-five years. But with most old properties, there will always be signs of damp somewhere, especially without adequate ventilation. Ideally, walls need to breathe. Air bricks allow this, but most old properties don't have them. Keeping air vents open in Upvc windows is a good way to let the air flow through. This cottage still had some damp in our living spaces. This is quite normal for older properties. Frank said it's nothing to be scared of, unless the walls were wet through. He said there is a way to keep any damp out of our living spaces, and that is to 'line out' the walls. Frank went on to line out and damp-proof membrane some of the external and internal walls, which I will talk about in subsequent chapters.

The new conservatory had a positive drying effect and warmed up the downstairs rooms. Plus, we had extra floor space and front row seats to view badgers, deer, foxes and rabbits visiting our garden.

At this time, we also insulated the loft space in the downstairs kitchen extension and upstairs main bedroom roof space. We firstly had to clear out straw that the Previous had used up there for insulation.

A romantic atmosphere.

A gentle walk up the lane
July 2010

Seeing, being close up to and experiencing more of the local wildlife, is the key to being at one with our environment. Delights and wonders are never far away.

I feel like we belong here in Mother Nature's garden. Like a keen synchronicity – we belong, we are part of the grass, we are part of the trees and we are part of all the animals too. Maybe I have finally gone insane, but that is absolutely fine because I feel close to many creatures, and anyone who has experienced this kind of lifestyle would probably understand. I don't think the animals mind us being here, so long as Jack or Kitty don't try to harm them.

I find hares fascinating. On Longs Lane, they don't know to run away, unless we tell them. They are fantastic, although from a distance, when you don't have glasses or a clear eyesight, they might resemble small Muntjac deer. (This is without an infusion of ginger wine!) This makes me smile because they can seem like a small dog too, just like the shape of a small Jack Russell, like Jack. There have been many times when I have called and called to 'something' in a field. I thought it was Jack, but after about seven or eight shouts and a hoarse voice, the animal, from being in a semi-frozen and flat position, jumps upright, raises his ears and then runs away like a bolt of lightning across the field. 'Wait a minute,' I think. 'Jack's ears aren't that long!'

The best times to see the hares are around 7 a.m. and 7 p.m. when they are foraging for food, playing around, standing tall and upright on their hind legs or bounding through the fields like miniature racehorses. But don't let these times be too fixed a routine because around here animals have no particular time frame at all, especially for visiting our garden – any part of the day will do, especially if we have unprotected cabbages, lettuce and whatever growing in the soil beds.

One year our garden was discovered by a hare (although it could have been a rabbit), who soon went to tell his friends. Within a few weeks we had virtually nothing left; they even visited our greenhouse too. Can you believe it, they didn't like the tomato and pepper plants, but loved to dig up the compost and rake through the roots underneath, thus destroying my tenderly home-grown seedlings. (We now have little two-foot-high wire gates at each greenhouse door and netting covering the crops in the soil beds. This seems to do the trick. However, if you should try this at home, please be careful not to forget the gate is there and fall over it when stepping into the greenhouse, just like we have on many occasions.)

I am not sure I would call hares beautiful; 'distinct' is probably more apt – a fine specimen of an athlete. I can remember once walking very quietly with Jack up our lane and slowing down at a secluded area where half of an old barn remains. Just around the corner, hares lope and rabbits graze. They seem unaware there is anyone or anything else around. I saw a hare one time and never in all my days have I seen such a 'cheeky chappie'. As I stood very still, there in front of us, about ten feet away, was a hare lying fully stretched out on his back, with his whitish brown fluffy tum on full display and his legs in the air. Was he sun bathing? This looked surreal! He was relaxing and enjoying the sunshine. His legs were limp and chilled and the back of his head and ears were touching the ground as he was reaching with his tongue to eat grass a few inches away. Instead of looking like a couch potato, he was a grass potato! Why bother getting up, if you can get what you need without moving? I liked his comfortable attitude. It was like watching someone enjoying a picnic and having everything right in front of them. I didn't want to disturb him, so we quietly crept away and strolled back down the lane.

A hare in our garden.

Hare playing in the rapeseed crop.

On one occasion, whilst I walked along our lane a little later in the year – around late September time – I met Madge, a nice lady from a nearby village, who was walking her dog. We shared our journey, only to be dismayed when we discovered a small bedraggled and puffy eyed creature looking up at us from the grass. It didn't move because it was nearly blind and we were able to walk right up to the poor little thing. It was a rabbit in the process of being devoured by myxomatosis. Its eyelids were huge and swollen and eyeballs thickly glazed over – a man-made horrendous cancer, now passed down through the rabbits, generation to generation. I felt a lump in my throat and then said to the rabbit, 'God bless you, I pray the Lord will take your soul to a kinder place.' I meant it with all my heart, for I hate to see animals suffer, especially for a drawn-out time and in lots of pain. Madge shared an empathic smile and then we both warned our dogs to leave it and let the creature be as we quickly walked on by.

I suppose living here, so close to nature, has altered the way I think and feel about animals and all manner of small creatures. Why is it now whenever something dies, however small, I feel a need to say a little prayer and send it off with a 'God bless you', and then have a feeling of wonder at whether God has taken its soul away before I leave it for other creatures to devour? I suppose I have learned to appreciate what we do have here on our doorstop and perhaps need to accept I can't make all these animals better – it's not my responsibility, it is part of Mother Nature's cycle of life.

During our walk together, Madge and I talked about crops in the fields, badgers, baking cakes, the village fete and lots of other things. Our dogs were walking on in front and our conversations took our attention from watching them closely, because on the way back down Longs Lane, Madge's dog found the poorly rabbit, picked it up and started to drag it around like a toy. The poor thing couldn't do anything and didn't stand a chance.

'Quick, I need a big piece of wood, a stone, a rock, a branch, something.'

'What???' I shouted back at Madge's urgency. 'Just tell your dog to leave it be – the fox 'ill take it!' I urged.

Madge was adamant; she rushed around to look for a weapon. What on earth was she planning?

I looked on in amazement.

Madge took a piece of wood that she found in the hedge and charged back over towards us like a raving maniac.

'Arrrgggghhhh.' She slammed the wood onto the poor rabbit's body.

'Arrggggghhhh.' And again!

'Arrrgggghhhh.' And again, with such force!

I felt sick to my stomach. I shouted, 'Madge, let Jack do it, he can kill quickly, he can do it – it'll be quicker.'

'No, the disease might harm him – no, now, out of the way, arrrgggghhh!' She held her arm out to keep me back, whilst with the other she continued to belt the already dead body.

What a strange woman she was.

Tears ran down my face and even the dogs cowered. I said my prayer out loud, 'God bless you, may the Lord take your soul to a kinder place.'

Madge and I walked home in silence. I didn't know how to question her or even what to say. The rabbit was certainly dead now.

As Madge and I reached the gate of Honeysuckle Cottage, we said our goodbyes and I went inside and told Frank all about it. I couldn't understand how someone could do such a thing; all I wanted was to leave it in the grass and let nature take its course. But Frank did point out to me Madge's possible reasoning behind her actions. She wanted to end its suffering too. But what gives anyone the right to take a life? I felt humble and insignificant in the event of being part of such a thing. So many animals and creatures die each day. As the farmer says, 'Wherever there is livestock, there's always deathstock too – it's just what happens and there's nowt much you can do about it'.

Everything that lives deserves life, not disease, especially not man-made disease. But that is my personal opinion. It's the way things are sometimes and it can take a great deal of courage to accept that something so beautiful can be made to suffer so much. But that's life. I have seen many a blackbird stolen from its nest by the hawk; the small bird screams for its life only to be taken away and eaten. I've thrown stones at them, to try and stop nature, but to no avail – the hawk needs to survive too.

The worst thing I have heard is the screaming sounds of death from rabbits and other animals but the fox needs to eat and the owl has its mate and young who would starve if he didn't take one or two animals from the hedgerow. On a lighter side, the most pleasant sound I hear nearly every day is from visiting pheasants to our garden, especially in late spring. The male pheasant will make lovely cooing sounds of approval when he picks up corn I have thrown down for him to eat. Then a few moments later, his shy lady companion will appear and follow his prompt to feed too. Recently, we had a male pheasant bring his lady with him and his little babies too. Shy at first, but so comforting to enjoy his moment of glory at discovering food for his family.

Percy pheasant and his lady-friend.

Is Honeysuckle Cottage haunted?

September 2010

There were times when I have not felt alone in this cottage, like we were sharing our home with someone or something. I'm not sure whether it's the character of the old place or whether we really have a presence. Bearing in mind that I do have quite a vivid imagination, it could all be in my head.

Our bedroom is part of the original house, and, as I mentioned previously, still has the original floorboards and low beamed ceilings. As you know, the room slopes downwards a few inches and until you get used to feeling like you're going to fall out of the window, it can seem a little strange. Quaint, but strange enough for a classic scene from a haunting.

During the winter of 2010, on a number of occasions, I felt that I was woken up repeatedly through the night by someone or something rocking my shoulder from side to side. On one occasion, though my eyes were reluctant to open fully, I caught a glimpse of the outline of something that looked like an old woman. Quickly dismissing this and being too tired to wonder whether it was a dream or not, I drifted back to sleep.

I told frank, and 'Edna' became our new joke. Frank would say, '...and how's Edna today then?' with a smile. I'd reply with something like, 'Oh, she's been busy helping me in the garden, planting flowers', to join in the fun.

But these episodes started to get serious if Frank had work the following morning and I had to be woken up during the night because I was moaning and crying in my sleep. Frank said I sounded like a woman possessed and seemed very frightened, so he felt it important to wake me. Then I would get angry at him for disturbing my sleep.

Frank would wake me with a start. I would get up, grunt at him, go to the loo and get straight back into bed.

'What on earth's the matter with you?' he said.

'I dunno, go back to sleep.'

'But, do you know what it's about?'

'Not sure, it'll settle down.' I replied, knowing full well that by the tone of my voice Frank would guess I really knew the truth. My Nanna had been taken into hospital again. It was a stroke. She was losing her mind too. Mum and Dad were not sure whether she had the beginnings of Alzheimer's or Dementia. When Maggie and I visited her, she couldn't remember us and it felt heartbreaking. So whether this 'haunting' had something to do with my upset, possibly so.

'I'm scared to go back to sleep.' I raised my eyebrows to try and keep my eyes open, but not for long. I drifted off into the night once more, but felt half awake and half asleep, like I was guarding myself.

I once looked up whilst sitting on the ensuite toilet to see an outline of Edna in bed beside Frank. Another time, I saw her leaning over him on the window side of the bedroom.

She looked dainty and frail, with an outline of what looked like long hair tied neatly in a bun at the back of her head.

What on earth was happening to me? I was frightened to sleep. My days were feeling more like nights and nights like days, all mixed into one. I went to see the doctor and asked him if it could be because I stressed about missing my family in Leeds. He gave me some pills and asked me to come back in a month.

I remember getting ready for bed with Frank one evening and jesting with him by saying something like, 'That Edna had better go and sort herself out tonight; I hope she knows we've got a gun!' Lo and behold, she must have heard us. For weeks nothing happened. We slept peacefully and the nightmares stopped.

But, a few weeks later it all started again. Edna was so persistent; she was now trying to pull my feet at the bottom of the bed. I started to feel as tired as I did when Maggie was a small teething baby. So enough was enough. Instead of running away from this 'ghost' or whatever it was, I decided to find out what she wanted from me...

It was like a scene from the Scrooge movie. The ghost of Christmas past comes to visit Scrooge and stands with him to show him all his family from times gone by, except this was about me.

Edna took a firm hold of my shoulder to pull me out of bed and, too tired to fight any more, I let her take my arm, and then she hugged me. I had a gut feeling deep inside that she had been trying to hold me all along and this is what she was trying to get through to me.

I don't know whether I was asleep or awake, but Edna led me downstairs. I remember thinking, 'Dear Lord, our house is a right mess!' Both Edna and I were looking around in the kitchen. I felt guided by her, I felt safe. I felt so very tired and worn. Yet, when we stepped nearer the living room, I could hear familiar voices. The door was half open, I couldn't see anything yet, but could hear voices I recognised from past times. It was Mum and Dad, Nanna, Auntie and Uncle and my brother. They were all sitting talking happily about anything and everything. Our neighbours were also in the house – they were teaching Maggie many useful things and especially how to be a local in the countryside. Everyone felt just as tired as me, even the neighbours, but they had much to teach. I felt relieved. My dream ended, I woke to hear birds singing outside in our garden.

I spoke to Mum the following day, but dared to tell her of these ridiculous imaginings or hauntings. Mum said to me, 'Sheila, I love you, and your Dad and I are so very proud of you.'

I threw the tablets away. That was the last I heard from Edna.

Before and after – upstairs, main bedroom and ensuite
November 2010

For around eight weeks, we slept on the mattress in our living room. It was the price we had to pay so that we could turn upstairs into a warmer and more comfortable place to sleep.

A picture of our main bedroom follows, before we changed anything:

The ensuite is behind the door in the picture. We had to remove this door because it was a balancing act each time we stepped out of the shower, also the toilet was only two feet away. Having a door restricted air flow, even though we had an electric fan, the walls were moldy in each corner. We had to get a plumber in to fix the broken Saniflow toilet, replace the dripping taps on the tiny sink, and plumb in a new shower. Again, we saved money by purchasing the shower on the internet ourselves. The shower cubicle was already fully tiled in white. So with Frank's creativity, he re-grouted the tiles with a quality dark grey grouting, and replaced a couple of broken ones. Frank also made a wooden box/shelf to cover the visible water pipes that ran along the floor and under the sink, at gable wall side, and fitted a mirrored vanity unit on the wall above and behind the toilet. I painted it with a good quality satin wood paint. I painted the gable wall with a specialist bathroom waterproof paint.

Since replacing the guttering outside, and having a new Upvc window in the bedroom, the internal walls had dried whilst we worked in the garden. But Franks was still keen to stop any potential damp from getting into our living space. He lined out that south-facing external wall and around the window with a damp-proof membrane and reformed the window reveal with timber, pine cladding. We painted the other walls with a good quality breathable emulsion in a warm light peach colour. To break up the ceiling, we painted the long pieces crisscross wood with a black matt paint. We then cleaned and stained the floorboards, and brought back our bedroom furniture from downstairs.

Here is the main bedroom once we had finished:

I love the bedspread, we bought it from a charity shop. There was a little patching in the corners that I finished off, but we thought it worked well with our countryside theme. Did you notice the long pillow that I made for the bedhead? This is the one that I made to keep us warm through the night.

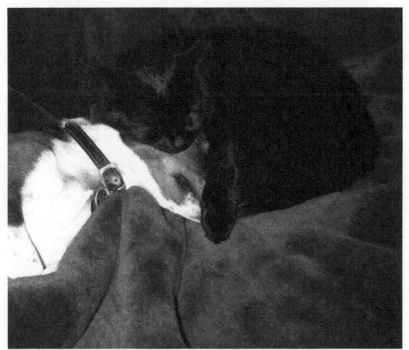

Kitty and Jack keeping warm.

The harshness of winter
December 2010

December 2010 was an exceptionally cold time; we had temperatures of minus fourteen and spent most of our time defrosting our chickens and their water. Chickens are usually quite hardy and can withstand cold and frosty weather but at minus fourteen, even being able to roost in their boxes was not enough to stop them from being frozen to their perches and too cold to get to their food. (We have since learned all about layering the hens' bedding – a natural composting way to provide heat for the hens in the winter. We also now put thick carpets over their roofs in sharp frosts too.)

We also saw our three-year-old gold fish get frozen to death in the pond. It was over two feet deep in places and it still froze solid.

We saw sparrows, pigeons and blackbirds eating dead relatives because they were hungry – there were not enough berries or food in the hedges. I know that those birds do not eat meat and it will be written somewhere that this really does not happen. However, if you come and live in the countryside during really bad weather, you can see it for yourself, and it is quite an upsetting sight. It was a case of eating dead meat or the creatures themselves dying.

Another harsh and desperate sight was at the large fish pond up our lane. This pond is around fifty yards square and has a steep embankment of around twenty feet, thus providing some shelter from the wind and bad weather. There are also brambles, hedges and weeds growing all around, to provide warmth and seclusion for badgers and foxes.

To exercise Jack, Frank and I walk up past this pond twice each day. It is around a quarter of a mile away on our long, straight unmade road. It is also very quiet because there are no other houses or dwellings apart from right at the end of the lane, where a family keep a small holding.

Each evening, this pond welcomes ducks to rest in reasonable safety until the next morning. Having said that, we know there are foxes and badgers, owls and hawks nearby. So, really, they need to stay on the water. We have seen many deaths near the pond because a bird has decided to roost in a secluded spot. The last one was a lone Canada goose that I tried to rescue – I could see its head and what seemed like its legs caught up in the hedge. After fighting through the brambles, I reached where it was, only to realise it had already been half eaten. From the lane, it looked as if it could have been saved and from where I was standing, it seemed to have its young alongside, but no, they were just bits of the bird itself strewn about the place. The poor thing had been torn to shreds.

One evening during the December 2010 snowy weather, we walked up past the pond quietly and heard a huge flock of ducks on the pond, quacking and settling down for the night. It was dusk and getting very cold. There was going to be another hard frost that night; we could feel it closing in.

We could feel the cold reach right through our clothes and into our bones. We could see the pond had started to freeze over already and the ducks were all huddled in the middle. Often where the ducks settle in the pond, it doesn't freeze over because of their continuous movement. It is the most naturally safe environment for them to be.

However, the next morning at 8 a.m. when we walked up the lane and reached the pond, the majority had flown, but there were still three or four left over. On the outskirts of where all the ducks had spent the night, these few ducks had frozen into the edge of the pond, the perimeter of the aforementioned huddle. The poor things experienced the cruel side of Mother Nature. Their bodies were no longer natural brown and fluffy white feathers. Pieces of them were dotted about the place, with small, red icy footprints leading towards the hedge and into the brambles. I felt sick to my stomach, but there was nothing we could have done. These poor birds had frozen into the edge because it had been so very cold; it was minus fourteen last night again. They got stuck overnight and the foxes had crept over to them and killed the defenceless things. What can I say, but this is life in the countryside. And as the farmers have said many times before, you can't have such a beautiful life without the harshness of death when it decides to come along.

Over the past years we have learned to respect Mother Nature and her values in this life. It's the cycle of life and we live right inside her magnificent beauty.

Before and after – second bedroom and stairs
February 2011

The following picture is the second bedroom before we made any changes:

On viewing day, the Previous had used a three-quarter cast iron framed bed to make the room look bigger. But when we tried this ourselves with a single bed, when we sat up we bumped our heads. So we think the bed was put in there to show an illusion of space. Those two little fitted wardrobes at each side couldn't fit a coat hanger in the traditional way, each piece of clothing had to be put in front of each other. This all looked pretty and romantic, but it was very impractical.

For nearly three years Maggie managed with a desk at the end of her bed and a free standing canvas wardrobe.

Traditionally, it's not a good idea to have a fitted wardrobe on an outside wall. But Frank had an idea to damp-proof membrane and insulate the wall, then to use thin polystyrene sheets before making a fitted wardrobe to fit around the window. The main bedroom had a fitted wardrobe all the way along the gable wall and this didn't prove to be a problem. (Frank drilled one-inch diameter ventilation holes along the bottom of each door, so it could breath.) He made a start:

During works, it was a difficult job for Frank with limited space. He designed and constructed a wardrobe from an uneven ceiling and floor, ranging from four feet high at one side to six feet high at the other side, at a sloping angle and to suit the bowed surfaces. Frank couldn't stand up straight to do this work. Everything had to be made upstairs because the steps are too narrow to get anything, other than tools and wood up there.

At this time, we couldn't afford to get the gable windows changed, so Frank made good around the window and we planned to get matching dark wood effect Upvc frames fitted as soon as we could save up the money.

He did it, the wardrobe was finished at last!

After Frank fixed a couple of the old wooden floor boards, we re-papered the ceiling and painted the walls with a refreshing light lemon breathable emulsion, and painted the woodwork with a good quality white satinwood paint.

Again, we found this Laura Ashley bedspread and curtains in a charity shop. I altered the curtains to fit and repaired the bedspread.

One of the newspaper reporters described this room as like a scene from Anne of Green Gables. And, Frank finished it at last, I felt proud of him, he worked really hard. As with everything in our Honeysuckle Cottage, it was never straightforward and often felt like our next test in life.

Now we had finished traipsing upstairs with paint pots, Frank could fix the creaking step:

We again used a good quality breathable emulsion paint for the walls. It would have been nice to have stair rods and an old fashioned carpet. But there would be less dusty corners to keep clean if we had a carpet. So we chose to have a mink plain Berber twist fitted:

It was a wonderful feeling when we moved our furniture back upstairs and put everything back in its place.

Our rescue diary of Percy
June to September 2011

Ducks, pheasants, blackbirds, wood pigeons, doves, and lots of different little birds, visit our garden because we put food out twice daily for our hens. We bought a bird table for the lawn and scattered a little corn and wild bird food there too. But once started, it had to be left every day because they came to rely upon us, especially during the winter months. One day we discovered a pheasant sleeping in the long grass at the bottom of our bird table. He was very timid, because when I approached, he quickly hopped into the brambles at the back of our garden. He was limping and looked as if he had been in the wars, perhaps fighting. Feathers were missing from his head and he kind of looked like he was going through a moult, but he was very weak and thin, and couldn't stand on his one good leg for very long. So we tried to help him in the hope he would grow stronger. I wrote these little bulletin updates:

3/6/11 – Percy doesn't hide from me, he's a wild animal, must be poorly. Saw him limping last night and we took the decision to let him be. If we take him to the vet, it might kill him with shock. He misses a day and then comes back another day. His ears are down and he has a few feathers missing from his neck. He looks a bit like one of my hens when they have been poorly. He is not plump like the other proud pheasants, and he hops along on his one thin leg. His other foot is swollen and tucked up near his belly. I wonder whether to give him some chick crumbs because they have a small amount of antibiotic in them. The mother in me wants to rescue him. But I stop myself and continue to throw him food. It saddens me, but many times we have tried to rescue injured animals, some die of fright. I suppose it's Mother Nature's way of saying, leave them alone. But Percy pheasant likes the food we keep on giving him, maybe he'll get stronger. Chopped up broccoli, grated carrot and grated apple, mixed with hen mash and chick crumbs. He's sheltering in the large umbrella plants at the back of our garden and sleeps at the bottom of our bird table at feed time.

11/6/11 (8 days later) – Percy arrives back at 4 p.m. It's been raining heavily, he is wet through, and goes to rest at the bottom of our bird table. He looks weak, his leg is red and swollen. But he does try to hide from me. This to me, means that he must have a bit of strength in him, otherwise he would be too weak to run away? I give him lots of food and some chick crumbs, and I make sure the water dish on the floor is full. He eats it all up, everything. After our own evening meal, I go out to the wash house and Percy is hopping in front of our conservatory and exploring the garden. This makes me feel happy. I would like to think Percy is looking for me, but he's getting around a bit. His leg is still not strong enough for him to walk on. Concerned, I go inside and search on the internet. I decide to try giving him an extremely small dose of ciprofloxacin antibiotic. I have a couple of leftover pills prescribed by my doctor. (Perhaps you shouldn't try this at home.) I divide them up into ten tiny amounts and mix the powder with his food twice each day. At dusk he makes several attempts to stretch his wings, no squawk though.

18/6/11(15 days later) – As I slowly kneel down, Percy makes several attempts to bend on his one leg and stretch out his wings. He jumps as high as he can and flies up on top of our shed. Hooray! This is the first time he has done this. Am feeling very proud because my efforts seem to be working. Something has been pecking at the back of his neck, or maybe he's been scratching? But how could he reach? Am still feeling positive about him right now. Thank goodness.

20/6/11 (17 days later) – Percy is back, it's 8.30am and I was going to clear algae out of the pond, but dash back to the greenhouse to fetch him some food. He's drinking the water we put on the floor by the bird table. His feathers are still very flat, his back is arched and his tail feathers are trailing on the floor. His ears are down, usually up and vibrant at this time of year. When I approach him to sprinkle food, he goes to hide. Again, this is a positive message, because he has the strength to move quickly, even though he's not yet fully fit. Also, Percy looks up attentively, alert, and around to listen to noises, this is the first time I have noticed him doing this. He rests his body on the floor and eats the food around him. But now he is managing to stand on his one good leg for longer, and lets his other leg touch the ground.

23/6/11 (20 days later) – This year we have masses of rabbits and baby bunnies. It goes from being lovely to see them all over the place to getting annoyed because they are eating all our plants. Now it's summer, and what was once a lovely picturesque garden is like a dying scene from Watership Down. It's like some kind of plague has taken them over. Mother rabbit is moving around slowly, her eyes are so swollen she can no longer see, she can't see her babies, they too are in the same state of health and they wander about aimlessly. Each time I go out to feed the birds, I wonder whether it might be kinder to kill the rabbits, go and get our gun and just shoot them all, but I have done enough of that kind of thing with rats, who am I to do such a thing. It's such a sad sight, the rabbits are getting thinner by the day and no longer run away from us.

30/6/11 (27 days later) – It's rained for days on end, not seen Percy today, but he came to visit last night. Oh the wonders, we had deer visit our gate this morning and then two deer in the field. Mixi rabbits are everywhere, poor things. Discovered newts in the pond! Our cat refuses to go outside because it is raining! This year we have many more ducks visit. Feeling excited because the coot we named Kevin is now nesting by our pond.

4/7/11(31 days later) – Percy's back and improving. I go outside to empty the bin and he's sat just outside the door. I nearly fall over him. He quickly hops away. I throw him some food. He looks old. His ears are down and even though his feathers are brighter now, I notice that his beak is curved and dull. But, he is trying to walk on both feet, with a little limp. The crows are unbelievable, because when I feed Percy, the crows and pigeons fight for the left overs. Today, a crow with three of her young were sat on my flowers, picking and eating them. They were playing with flower petals. When I reach for my camera, they fly away. No doubt they will be back for more when my back is turned. For the past two days we've had visits from a mallard and his lady friend. He's sat by our fence, like he ordered burger and chips or something. He's staring at me, watching and waiting. So when I go out to the greenhouse, I can't help but get him a cup full of bird feed. And guess what? Yes, that is what he wants. Now I have created another rod for my back and another place to put food each day. Soon we will be eating beans on toast every day because I spent all our housekeeping on wild bird food.

A mallard and drake pruning themselves after taking a swim in our pond.

10/7/11 (37 days later) – I rush home from the charity shop to feed the birds and frighten Percy. I didn't expect him to be sat in the full sunlight under our bird table, but he was. It's now nearly half three, I usually feed the birds at two. I'm late, and he is reminding me. It's been raining lots for the past week. Percy's head feathers have now fallen out and he looks like a completely bald Fryer Tuck. He can stand on his weak foot and hop a little. Have decided he must be an old bird, his beak is large and twisted and he looks worn, the poor thing. I might see if there are any vitamins I can mix with the bird feed to try and help him get a little stronger.

15/7/11 (42 days later) – Not seen Percy for a few days, hope he is okay. I keep on renewing the bird feed. Flippin' crows, eating it all! They bring all their family, great big things. One crow with five of her young, and they keep on taking it in turns to sit on the bird table and jump up to break off a piece of the coconut half that I stuffed with goodies. The crows even frighten the starlings and try to stop them from feeding their young. Also, when I put food out now, they don't wait for me to walk away, they just fly out in front of me, bullies!

16/7/11 (43 days later) – Percy pops out from the back of our garden. The temperature is really hot, about seventy degrees this afternoon. Percy usually waits until late afternoon, but I think he must be hungry. I put some food down for him, he eats, and off he goes again. About half two, I take Jack for a walk. No one would believe me unless I took the pictures. But I don't care, I know I saw it and you can think what you want. But I saw a stoat cross our lane with three of her young trundling along behind her. Like a school crossing patrol, she ushered them quickly back into the hedge at the other side of the lane. Startled, I again looked on in amazement and a great big happy smile spread across my face. Mother Nature has done well this year. We have seen so many animals with their young. The climate is not what it used to be when I was young, in the 1970s, when we had a summer at summertime and winter at wintertime. It keeps on being scorching hot and then thunderstorms, continuous rain for around two to three days, and then the heat is on again, and so on. We can see the garden growing faster than I can write these words!

30/8/11 (57 days later) – A wonderful surprise today, I see a barn owl on my way home from Louth, he's scanning the dykes. This is the first time I have spotted one for over a year. All the barn owls we used to see around our cottage seem to have disappeared. But it was lovely to be reminded of their graceful presence. At home, looking over to the chicken pen, I see a pheasant that appears to have a golden crown. The more I look at him the more I realise it isn't golden, it's the sunlight shining on his bald patch, poor old thing. It's Percy, he has managed to jump over the fence. He is trying to get his share of the hen feed. I am guessing that seeing him less frequently could mean that he is managing better on his own. He's invented his own 'silly walk', he can fly and jump! I hope he gets through the remainder of the summer. The winter will be a testing time for him. But at least we've given him the opportunity to get through another few months.

5/9/11 (63 days later) – This afternoon we saw Percy using his poorly leg to scrat on the ground for food. Very lightly, but he's doing it. Been weeding in the garden and watching him. He's getting back that boldness, his feathers are shining in the sunshine, even his bald head! Percy's doing well, seen him flap his wings and heard him making noises. Percy has found his voice, feeling really happy.

22/9/11 (80 days later) – Percy's taken to sleeping by our pond with the visiting ducks, oh we love him. His bald patch looks smaller, feathers are growing at last. He stands at the pond and watches me, waiting for a delivery of food. But I've reduced it to once a day now so he will forage more often. Everyone's getting one feed per day, I'm not a zoo keeper! These animals need to learn about independence!

27/9/11 (85 days later) – Not seen Percy in a few days. Frank arrives home from work and tells me that he had to stop for a limping pheasant at the end of our lane. Frank reports Percy is looking good, and proud.

Percy.

Before and after – the living room
September 2011

Here are pictures of the living room before we completed any work:

After we had the conservatory fitted, Frank removed the external glass panelled doors, lined and damp proof membraned the south facing external wall and plastered it. After cutting out rotten pieces of wood and using a good quality filler, he painted the external doors with four coats of Weathershield gloss. This is a brilliant paint, top quality. In a beautiful red velvet colour, they made the living room look more attractive. Once the paint had dried, the doors were tougher and difficult to damage, even with the clumsiest of knocks.

Frank reassured me that even though the cottage has a damp proof injection along each of the external walls, guaranteed for 25 years, the areas of damp were nothing to be concerned about. He said damp areas are expected in a property of over 150 years old. Again he used damp-proof membrane and v-groove wood panelling to line under the window and around to the fireplace. Near the kitchen door, he made a wood bookcase, lined it, and then fixed it to the wall. Our living room was warmer and dryer, and it could breathe because we painted the walls with a good quality breathable emulsion.

Summer in October

October 2011

Last night we had our first frost of the year. It was white everywhere this morning and a blanket of icy wet cotton wool fog covered the fields.

The weather has been strange lately; the temperature today was in the twenties with a clear blue autumn sky. We have strawberries waiting to turn red for the second time this year and some flowers are back in full bloom too. Lavender had already flowered in June but now it's flowering again. All the other plants in our garden are taking it in turns at getting another chance to bloom. We have spinach and beetroot growing and a great big pumpkin just holding on for its final week before we cut it to make a lantern. There are butterflies and bees galore. It really is like summer in the autumn!

A wild rose.

Before and after - the downstairs bathroom
November 2011

The downstairs bathroom walls were already lined out and the floor laid with quarry tiles. Apart from filing gaps to stop Mother Nature's creatures from getting inside, we just redecorated.

Before and after – the old kitchen
November 2011 to January 2012

Pictures of the dining area with kitchen in the background (before any changes):

Basically Frank ripped out everything from the old kitchen and started again.

As with other rooms in the cottage, walls that had signs of damp, he lined with damp proofing. This reduced any moisture from getting into our living space and provided a good insulation.

We had enough money to pay for our gable windows at this time, so Frank carefully and sensitively took out the old ones and worked with a local contractor to put in wonderful draught-free Upvc frames. He had to be careful because there were no stone lentils above or underneath to hold the house bricks in place and it became like a game of catch-the-falling-brick. But once the frames were fitted, we patched and decorated around them and sealed any difficult gaps with a setting spray foam. It was a relief to be able to have our new windows open on the draught without having flies invade our space.

At an antique shop in Horncastle, we fell in love with a quaint sixteenth century double cupboard. This 1750s piece of history became our new magical Narnia cupboard. Frank fitted it neatly under the kitchen chimney breast and continued the tongue and groove wood panelling to the wall.

Next, we had an electrician take down the fluorescent lighting and put in a temporary light whilst Frank prepared the ceiling.

Frank designed and scribed wooden beams to the bowed ceiling by ripping straight pieces of wood to fit.

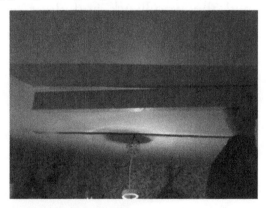

The ceiling was uneven, Frank took his time to measure and adjust the wood to suit.

He also made a new ledge and brace door for the bottom of the stairs – entrance into the old kitchen. Then he filled all the loose powdery cement holes in the floor. The electrician returned and fitted ceiling spot lights. A plumber replaced old external water pipes around the old sink area and fitted a stop tap with a mineral ball filter.

We painted the paneling with a good quality satin wood paint and stained the woodwork and door adjoining the stairway with a ten year guarantee wood satin varnish.

Finally there was a perfect place for our old pot sink...

Another walk up the lane
January 2012

At 6.50 a.m. on a wet January morning, Jack and I take a walk along Longs Lane. With no street lights, we are guided by last night's full moon. My eyes soon become accustomed to the half-light. Puddles have started to dry in the breeze. For a worm, it could be the worse day of his life – can he reach damp soil before shriveling up? I rescue a few, placing them underneath leaves, then I walk further along. Pulling my scarf closer to my neck, I stop as a hare jumps out of the hedge. Slowly, I lift Jack into my arms and stand very very still. The hare stops, has a sniff of the soil, and then hops a little closer, and sniffs some more. Next, he actually sniffs my trainers! How wonderful to be so close. But I guess the smell of my feet gives off a pong, because he realises I am not a tree and runs away.

At this time of year we may see foxes, badgers, owls, rats, pheasants and, lucky for us, a pair of buzzards circling the trees tops. Sad to say, the usual reason for seeing these animals is because they are hungry and looking for food. They're not playing out like me. The fox has its family to feed and will look for an unwary rabbit, hare or pheasant. The barn owls will be pairing up sometime soon – the male barn owl has to work very hard to prove himself every day and bring back lots of food, like mice and whatever he can catch. Then the female will believe him to be a good match. All the pheasants and birds search for anything they can find; occasionally, hidden deep in the undergrowth, the odd berry remains on a hawthorn bush or bramble.

A barn owl flies towards us. He is gliding along the dykes and gullies searching for prey. Like a cotton wool cloud with wings, he drifts silently. Again, we stand very still. He glides by smoothly, with grace.

Quick over there, in the field! A fox looks like he's running sideways, as if he is River Dancing across the mud. He sees us. He stops for a moment to figure us out. He looks on with his red and drooling mouth, teeth showing. Jack's fur stands on end. I wonder if the fox is going to approach, but he flies off, looking back to check we are not a threat.

I wouldn't swap these experiences for the world. We have made our mark on this Longs Lane, the wild animals know we too share this land, our scent is familiar. At least that is what I would like to think in my fairytale mind.

Refreshed, we arrive back at our Honeysuckle cottage's five bar gate. Quick as a flash, a sparrowhawk speeds down like a jet. I feel her wind just above my head. She has flown straight into the hedge and taken a blackbird. There is no sound. The hens look up. The ducks look up. Everyone knows, but dare not say. Accepting this crude event, I turn to see that rabbits have been digging in our garden to the size of badgers holes. Instead of getting mad, I feel enthused. I fetch a bucket and collect the fine soil for compost.

Longs Lane, facing South.

Longs Lane, facing North.

Windy times
4th and 5th January 2012

Four and a half years after moving into Honeysuckle Cottage we are used to the windy weather; with our land being flat and open, we often get the brunt of a bad storm. Especially since lowering the height of our perimeter trees. Even the first week we moved here, we watched as huge trees moved from side to side, just like tent pegs squishing in wet mud, we wondered whether they were going to blow away – or in the case of our trees, blow down and fall through the cottage roof.

The TV forecast earlier in the week had given out a severe wind warning. But by now, we felt hardened to bad weather; we felt we could handle anything. However, last night the hurricane-like wind quickly found us and the force was tremendous. It was blowing so hard we felt as though the cottage was moving – the doors and windows were rattling like anything. I went outside late at night to check on things in our garden and the glass panes in the greenhouses were also rattling like mad. I felt unnerved, especially when all three chicken houses were being lifted off the ground by the gusts and dropped back down again with a thud, even though I had put bricks on top to weight them down. At our gate, I could see the electricity cables swaying, and the old junction box very near to the room we were going to sleep in was making loud and unusual buzzing noises.

Our little two-berth caravan wasn't fixed down

and it too was swaying with the force, right next to our car – we wondered if it might roll over, but there was nothing we could do, just hope the damage would be minimal. Overall, things felt pretty scary outside, so I dashed back into the house and hoped for the best.

Our cottage entrance door still had the long door curtain and thick blanket inside the frame. It covered the whole of the door and the cat flap too. It was effective, during really cold and windy weather. But the winds at this time were so strong that the cat flap was blowing open and then shut again. There was really no point in protection being there at all. We could feel a gale blowing through the kitchen and dining room. So after a short time, we lock the cat flap and bring Kitty's cat litter tray inside the kitchen. Not ideal, but there was no way she wanted to go out in the cold, especially when she found her warm and cosy cushion next to the radiator. But still, the only way we could keep our feet and legs warm (because of the huge gaps underneath each internal door) was a thick pair of woollen socks and a warm blanket wrapped around our lap. Alternatively, we could avoid some of the draught if we put our feet and legs up on the sofa to keep warm.

In the living room, we have large velvet curtains hanging at the double glass panelled doors which lead into the new conservatory. On the other side of those doors we have another rail with another pair of long, thick velvet curtains. However, we could still feel the raw weather flowing right through our home.

We didn't get much sleep that night, with Jack barking at every noise outside along with our own thoughts of what damage we were going to find in the morning. In fact, we had no quality sleep at all.

By early morning it was still very windy and I reluctantly took Jack for a short walk along our lane. I watched the huge trees still moving about and the thought of those swaying electricity cables and an image of them snapping and sending electric currents along the ground made me rush Jack on to do his toilet so we could get back in the warm.

On the way back, we had a good look at our roof and it seemed OK. I let the hens out of their boxes and noticed that the far greenhouse had been pushed sideways by about a foot, with a few panes of broken glass. There was glass all over the place. Also, another piece of glass had smashed and fallen inside and all over our plant pots. There were bits and pieces of plants and glass everywhere.

Later in the morning, we needed to go and buy groceries from our local supermarket, about ten miles away in Louth. On the way, I can remember seeing lots of fences blown down, signposts blown over and trees uprooted. I saw a house with so much damage; its roof had been blown off. It honestly looked like a small hurricane had swept through the town.

When we watched our local news and weather that evening there were reports and pictures of a huge beech tree fallen in Grimsby, and in Spalding, walls had been blown down.

Apparently, the severest wind was about sixty-nine miles per hour, recorded in Scampton. In Lincolnshire alone, around seven thousand homes lost their power and across our region, no fewer than sixty trees had blown down too. In Willoughby, a village near us, a stable had been blown high into the air, right out of a field. It took flight and blew over the road and into a dyke.

Minus sixteen!
11th February 2012

This is Jack wearing his knitted coat. It was too cold for his walk:

Longs Lane was frozen solid. That morning, there was not a sound or movement anywhere:

Never in all our five years here have we felt cold like this. On the 11th February 2012 I got up at the usual time of 6 a.m. and absolutely everything outside was white, frozen in animation, with icicles too. I couldn't get the cottage door open without great force. The moment I stepped outside, my hair froze white. I was wearing a hat, but the bits of hair sticking out froze white, as did my eyebrows, chin, cheeks, lips and tongue. I was outside for only five minutes. Our hens were well and truly stuck in their roosting boxes. I gave up trying to free them in minutes because as I knelt down the intense pain from the cold seeped through my clothes and into my bones. My fingers could not move either, even though I wore thick gloves. Also, Jack needed to be taken for his walk, or so I thought...

Jack and I managed to get only a short way before I could barely walk and he would not walk either. Kitty (as usual) followed us a short way behind and all the tips of her once black fur turned white – just like she had been brushed with paint. I ushered them both back home and we got the fire burning well with the central heating on full. It was too dangerous to be outside.

Over the page is the minus 16 temperature reading from our car at 9.08 am. I guess it was pretty accurate:

At around 11a.m., armed with a small bucket of warm water and sponge, I decided to try and open the hen boxes by wetting them, but the water froze on contact. It was still minus eleven. It seemed like a good idea to leave them be for a short while in the hope the temperature would improve. Even by mid-afternoon it was only minus eight, but I did manage to get the poor things out to feed them. I found it amazing that our hens could get through these sub-zero temperatures. But we did take precautions. We used really thick woollen rugs, entirely covering each of their boxes and held on top by old house bricks. Inside, the boxes were packed with layers of straw, hen poo and wood shavings. (A technique that a local small holder taught me.) These had been composting well since late September and the smell was not too bad so it didn't affect their breathing. It just kept them warm.

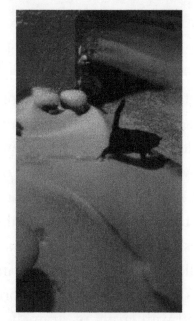

Kitty, investigating the snow.

Taking flight
3rd January 2012

It's now 9 a.m. on Tuesday 3 Jan 2012 and I've just been for a walk along Longs Lane with Jack – it is extremely windy. I am five feet seven inches and weigh nearly ten stone. I jumped up in the air like a star and the wind blew me a foot backwards!

Surrounding fields in winter.

In spring, daffodils decorate Longs Lane.

Heavy Snow
5th February 2012

Before and after – the old dining room
April 2012

Here is the old dining room before any changes:

Once our kitchen was fitted, we could brighten up this room and enjoy the open countryside view through each of the windows...

Firstly, Frank removed the old wallpaper. It was glued on, not with ordinary paste, but with some kind of electric steamer resistant glue. It took him a very long time to remove every last piece of those busy Wm Morris peaches and pomegranates. But he eventually did it. No surprises there – everything felt like a test! But, once our Frank makes up his mind, he achieves. That's what I love about him, sheer fool-hardy determination to finish whatever he starts.

We had a plumber come along for two visits, firstly to move the radiator, freeing the space for our kitchen cupboards, and secondly to do the plumbing for our Belfast sink and taps. We had a generous space to plan our countryside kitchen:

All the time, trying to find the best for our money, and being on a fairly tight budget, we searched until we eventually found an advertisement on Ebay: Back in Yorkshire, there was a skilled man with a workshop in his garden. He made bespoke pine kitchen cupboards. We loved them, they were just what we had in mind, simple, plain and bold. Once the man had finished our order, he delivered them. We made him tea and cakes and thanked him for his hard work with payment and a few jars of homemade jam.

Our new kitchen was going to have sunshine yellow walls with chunky pine cupboards...

So, like the old kitchen area, Frank designed and scribed wooden beams to the ceiling by ripping straight pieces of wood to fit. We painted them matt black and put hooks in them, ready to hang baskets and drying herbs from our garden. We had an electrician come along and fit spot lights on the ceiling. Next Frank replaced missing and damaged skirting boards, constructed a new wooden cupboard to house the central heating boiler, and refitted and made good the cottage stable-style external wooden door until we could afford to buy a new dark wood grain effect Upvc one.

Frank fitted the units and worktops to the wall. The pine was treated with a soak-in stain, but we still bought a table top protector and covered it with a plastic gingham table covering. (About a year later, Frank had an idea to varnish the worktops with a strong and good quality matt yacht varnish. This made the surfaces more hardwearing.)

We had a good quality linoleum fitted to the floor:

At last! Our Honeysuckle cottage was finished.

Home-made produce seemed the natural thing to do.

Wettest April on record
April 2012

We have had lots of rain over the years and I can safely say, even during the heavy rains of July 2007 and April 2012, we have not flooded. Our lane is unmade and the potholes fill to the brim with water:

Frank has continued to ensure any large puddles next to our property can drain through to his dug-out trenches and into the lane-side dyke. The drainage board come along once a year and dredges out this main drain.

But, oh, the mud! Especially after harvest and during winter months.

Air-sea rescue

May 2012

I imagine May and June 2012 must have been the wettest months on record; it rained nearly every single day. There was still a hosepipe ban here in Lincolnshire because we had had such a dry winter and the land was not getting enough rainwater to fill the reservoirs either. Talk about dampening the spirits, everyone we spoke to moaned about the weather. Our nation is good at complaining about it being too hot, too cold, too wet or too windy, but this time there was a valid reason. The rain was very intense and torrential, even with hailstones the size of small golf balls on one occasion that smashed car windscreens in a local supermarket car park.

In the past years, our drains and dykes have been tested thoroughly with extreme weather, but they have always proved their worth; Honeysuckle Cottage and its garden has never flooded. But the May and June rain in 2012 continued to be persistent. I think the weather forecasters on TV must have cringed at having to repeat, each and every day, that we were going to get more rain. I wonder whether they ever received hate mail? Goodness knows what the weather must have done to the crops growing in the farmers' fields. I guess it will have affected growth, the fields were waterlogged long enough for ducks to make their home there. But we didn't let the weather get us down. On Thursday 28th June, we had a table booked for an evening meal at our favourite country pub, the Blacksmiths Arms in Skendleby. The landlord, landlady and staff are friendly, and originally from our home county of good old Yorkshire. To us, going there for a meal is much like coming home for tea with tasty home-made food and a welcome cheery smile. However, on this particular Thursday we were concerned at the very heavy rain and whether it might affect their opening times, so we made a mental note to telephone and check before venturing out.

Thursdays are grocery shopping days. We usually go out mid-morning. But because the weather forecast had given out a warning for a potentially dangerous electrical storm later in the day, we decided to be out of the house by 9am to fetch the groceries as soon as we could.

Driving along our lane we saw a man we didn't recognise walking on his own, slipping and sliding and trying to avoid the puddles. He was wearing smart trousers and a jacket, with trainers, in the thick mud? So we stopped to warn him. 'Hello there, best watch you don't get wet through?' The man grunted as a reply, so I said, 'Yeah, there's a bad storm coming this afternoon.' He looked at me blankly. I took a deep breath, turned to look at Frank and chuntered under my breath, 'What's the matter with him then?' Frank leaned back into his seat and shrugged his shoulders. Closing the car window we drove off and continued into the village and headed for the main road.

By around 11a.m., the sky started to look like a scene from a disaster movie. It was very dark, and the atmosphere was eerie, humid and still. Hurrying, we dashed around the shops and made our way home. By this time, large droplets of rain had started to hit our windscreen, though with the humidity, they dispersed just as quick. But we could feel something brewing in the air, and the sky looked like it was going to explode.

When Frank got out of the car to open our gate, I drove in and he motioned me to look up north of where we were. Because our land is very flat, we can see for miles and it is often easy to spot bad weather approaching. On this day, we could see lightning striking and thick black storm clouds on their way towards us. So as quickly as we could, we bundled the shopping into the house and switched the kettle on for a cup of tea. Within minutes, it absolutely poured it down and down and down. I dashed outside to put our hens away because the rain and hailstones was so heavy it could have harmed them. The force of these water droplets mixed with hail, bruised the back of my head. It was like being pounded with golf balls. Kitty shot through the cat flap like a bullet. She looked like she had been swimming in the pond. Frank and I each took a towel from the airing cupboard and went to dry ourselves in the living room, looking out through the conservatory, and watched in amazement. Within fifteen continuous minutes of torrential rain, our garden was completely waterlogged. In this next picture, you can see the bottom panel in our conservatory door - the water was only a short way from flooding our cottage. In this picture there was eight inches of surface water filling the sunken patio:

'What we gonna do, we can't go out to the Blacksmiths and leave this!' I worried. 'It's only early yet, don't worry, we can always give 'em a ring and check they're still open.'

'Yes, but what about this...look! How can you stay so calm?' I said, pointing to the paddling pool in front of the conservatory doors.

'Stop it love, remember, I dug out a soakaway, it'll be alright.'

Within half an hour the rain storm had slowed and almost stopped. Jack needed to go for his walk.

Honeysuckle Cottage looked like it had been plonked in the middle of a pond. Looking at the sky I decided it was going to be dry enough to take Jack for a short walk. I stopped briefly to watch a helicopter in the distance. I thought it strange he was hovering around a village near us. 'Looks like something is happening over there Jack – hope they're OK. Maybe someone's being rescued?' Our dog looked up at me and tilted his head. I translated it as an 'Mmm, yes Mummy.'

I could see a small figure in the distance, and thought it was our neighbour. I stretched up my arm and gave a great big friendly wave, just like we normally exchange in recognition at seeing each other. I presumed he or she was from the village. But this time, our 'neighbour' didn't wave back and I felt a bit hurt and ignored. 'I wonder what's the matter with them then,' I mumbled. Jack and I started back down the lane, and the figure, which I could now tell was that strange grunting man from earlier. He appeared to be walking towards us. 'Maybe he wants a word, Jack.' But my attention was taken away by the fast approaching helicopter. I speed-walked Jack the rest of the way back home to fetch Frank who was standing watching TV in the living room.

Before I could speak he said, 'Have you seen this, Sheila, there's a news flash on, it's been really bad...'

'Wow, look at that, Frank.' I pointed towards the TV. 'The flooding is terrible, those poor people...hey, you'd better come outside, Frank, and take a look at what I've seen.'

'What are you talking about?'

'There's an air-sea rescue helicopter flying near, Look,' I said pointing out of the living room window.

We could see the helicopter, flying about and getting lower and then rising again just missing our electricity cables. Both Frank and I went to stand at our cottage door as it reached the top of our flooded garden. I could feel my heart thumping as we both wondered what the helicopter was searching for. This G-force hair dryer made me hold onto my head whilst trying to look up at the crew who were leaning out of their open door.

'Frank!' I shouted loudly, because of all the noise, 'What do you think they want? Had we better tell them we're alright?' We must have looked so stupid. It was probably obvious to anyone other than us that they were searching for that wondering and grunting man, but we had forgot about him and thought they were coming to our rescue!

Now Frank was starting to join in with my hysteria and said that the usual thing to do in these situations is to give a thumbs-up to say we are OK. He said he had seen it done in the films and rescue programmes on TV. So we agreed promptly to give a great big sky-reaching thumb in the air to let the pilot know we are OK even though the garden looked like a swimming pool. The helicopter crew waved back at Frank's hand signal and flew to the south of our house ... but then, they started to get even lower. 'Oh no! What are they doing, Frank? What have you gone and done? It looks like they're gonna land in the field.' And that is just what they did, right at the side of our cottage. Oh the embarrassment! Why didn't they recongise our thumbs up?

'Oh the stress!' I said to Frank, pushing him off the door ledge, 'Oh no, Frank, what are we going to do? Go and apologise, Frank, go and tell them we are alright, we're going to look such fools. How much is this gonna cost us then? We'll get fined you know for bringing them down. Go and tell them Frank, please!'

I turned and bent down with my teeth gritted and said one or two swearwords whilst stamping my feet. What fools we were. Frank dashed out through our gate to try and sort out the misunderstanding. He was being blown sideways like a dated 1970s police rescue film. A policeman and medic climbed out of the cabin. I could see them chatting about something, but tried to hide behind the corner of our hedge, embarrassed at what we had caused.

By now, the farmer and his wife were running up the lane towards us and shouting, asking if we were alright. 'Are you alright, Sheila?' he shouted. Although, to be honest, I think they wanted to get a close-up of a real life rescue helicopter.

'Oh yes, thanks, I think so... we've got a bit of situation here and it's seems to have escalated.' Who did I think I was, a rising star from some kind of Skarsky and Hutch episode?

The farmer, his wife and I stood at our gate in the hot post-rain sunshine and discussed the past couple of hours and the terrible downpour. Their cattle shed and farmyard was completely flooded, but their house was safe. I showed them around our garden, but by now the water was starting to drain away. Thank goodness Frank was correct about his soakaway.

Frank was busy shaking hands with the policeman and the crew were getting back on board the helicopter. He waved them off and returned to tell me about the grunting old man. Apparently, he lived in the next village and had decided to take himself for a little walk and had been wandering for two days. The poor man suffered from Dementia and didn't know what he was doing. But thanks to the air-sea rescue he was safely taken back home again. Most folk have to pay for that once-in-a-lifetime thrill at the seaside, but this dear man got a ride in a helicopter for free. Not that he would care; after my interrogation and the heavy rain, I am sure he was very pleased to get back home again and be reunited with his worried relatives.

Later in the afternoon we rang our favourite country pub, the Blacksmiths Arms, to see if they were still open and their reply was, 'Of course we are, we look forward to seeing you – you're very welcome!' Great, we thought, time to go out and relax to get away from all this madness and the strange surreal life we lead. We arrived for 6.30 p.m. and had a relaxing drink and a very tasty home-cooked meal amongst pleasant company.

Mother Nature's creatures
Warning! Photographs of beetles, spiders, slugs and
moths (plus other cute & cuddlies)
May 2012

A strange looking moth in our garden.

A giant hornet.

A hairy caterpillar.

Huge water beetles from our pond.

Slugs galore.

Bunnies in our garden.

Curious young bulls.

Percy the pheasant.

Earl grey, our lavender silkie bantam cockerel.

A young bantam cockerel eating a piece of apple.

Rescuing Oscar
August 2012

Oscar was a young male hunting bird who hurt his wing during strong windy weather 25/26th August 2012. We rescued him for a few days - fed him well and kept him warm and dry until he could fly away safely. He gripped my hand:

Oscar flew from my hand and onto the old dustbin...

...then, he flew into his tree, looked back, as if to say goodbye – then he flew away:

Chicken zoo 3
September 2012

Here are George and Mildred again. They were delightful:

They were the best pets we'd had, and comical to watch. Both liked to be stroked. The owners hand-reared them and they were very tame, friendly and sociable with the hens. George was a bit randy and liked to do his thing very regular. Poor Mildred had to submit, until he left her alone for a month to hatch out some fertile eggs. Then, he waited patiently, until Mildred brought out her babies and he celebrated being a daddy by helping her by gently nuzzling them and wagging his tail in excitement.

I would recommend this experience to anyone thinking of keeping hens or ducks. Although I feel it's important to have a good plan of how to make your broody safe and comfortable, what time of the day (or every other day) you're going to lift her off the eggs to make sure she eats something and goes to the toilet away from her nest. Also, to decide what you are going to do with the ducklings/chicks once they are old enough to leave mum. Especially if you don't manage to sell them all. However, the mother hen or duck is a curiosity, especially watching her bring her young out of the nest box for the first time and teaching them to feed. The hen curves and arches herself, providing a safe canopy for her chicks to hide underneath and keep warm:

The mother duck waddles from her nest with her ducklings close behind, leading them out to their very first adventure.

However, again, for us, duck keeping was not to last. We let George and Mildred hatch out their young, and a few months later sold the ducklings and then gave the adults to the farmer up the road, who had lots more of them besides. We felt we didn't have enough room for them all. Also, George insisted on trying to roost in the trees. It was really hard work persuading him back into the pen every single evening.

I would say this, unless you have lots of room, with a big pond, and are not bothered by the noise, mud, poo and smell everywhere, ducks are definitely a 'no no', even though they are delightful to have around, especially when you see them having a bath in the pond and tending to their young. The difference between keeping hens and ducks, for me, is the mess. With hens, wearing garden gloves, I collect the hen poo each day from within the wood shavings just below where the hens roost; it is usually a solid consistency and this is a quick and easy task. Put the poo either straight on the roses or compost, and wash your hands, done! With ducks, you need a hosepipe, a bucket and scrubbing brush or something similar because their poo is very watery, and this is normal for ducks.

*

Eventually we saved only one of our bantam hens. She was a cross-breed, small ginger and very tame. So we had a look on the internet and decided to order some hatching eggs for her to raise as her own. They arrived in the post in a solid polystyrene container, with the six eggs packed safely inside. We paid around £15 for these six hatching eggs including postage. They were miniature bearded Silkie bantams. When they arrived we left them to stand in a quiet place, still in their box, for around twenty-four hours. In the meantime, over the next few days we had not been removing the hen's eggs from her nesting box and she had decided not to leave them either. She had become settled, spreading herself out and looking protective on her bed of warm, clean straw, free from any draughts. Two days after the hatching eggs had arrived, I decided to put them underneath our now broody hen. I chose to wait until it was nearly dark one night because hens go mellow and placid around this time, when they are about to roost for the evening. It was easy to slip my hand carefully and slowly underneath her feathers and take the few eggs which were underneath her and replace them carefully with our six new hatching eggs. She then shuffled herself and moved the new eggs back underneath her body.

The eggs took around twenty-one days to hatch and during this time I made sure that she got off her nest to eat once a day, and toileted away from her nest. At around fourteen days I candled the eggs (that is checking to make sure they are all fertile and therefore should hatch). There is lots of information in books and on the internet about how to do this with a home-made shoe box and a light bulb, but I found the easiest and most effective way was to stand in our pantry (which is pitch black anyway) with our torch, hold the egg at the top, shine the torch through it and if the egg was not see-through, then it was very probably fertile. Bad eggs can cause damage, so it is always best to make sure they all have something growing inside.

I also covered the whole of the roof of the pen with plastic pea netting and checked the perimeter for any gaps, to make sure any rats, mice, stoats or weasels could not get into the pen. Then I let Mother Nature take its course. The mother hen knew exactly what to do and for the last few days we knew something was happening because she wouldn't get off her nest to feed. Then on the twenty-fourth day, up she rose, and when the hatchlings were just forty-eight hours old, she brought them outside her box, looking like a feathery hovercraft with legs, carefully protecting her young.

We settled with these miniature bantam silkies because they can be very tame. (There are a couple of fun videos and lots of uploaded pictures on our Facebook page, We Love Lincolnshire Countryside if you would like to take a look.) These hens can't fly (or jump high) because their feathers have more of a downy texture. They do go broody very easily, but also lay a regular supply of eggs, even through the winter. Most hens stop laying eggs during the cold weather, but not these. The silkies are comical and pleasant to watch. We have enough room to keep them in our coop because they are small and we have the choice of letting them into the field for a few hours too. They never stray far or try to get into our garden; they delight in eating a little grass and making small dust baths in sheltered areas around our perimeter. We also found it easier to cope with these hens in the winter, especially when the temperature was extreme, as they could be kept inside our small shed (obviously with food and water) for a day or two with only a few hours out in the pen. So from our unrealistic and romanticised view of keeping hens and ducks, we finally settled on these miniature bantam silkies.

Even though we thought long and hard, we still made mistakes, which I am sure is quite normal. We learned such a lot from our hen and duck keeping, especially our late and wonderful team of Offenders. They were a great way to start off and it does feel rather uplifting knowing we were responsible for giving Pecky Sue and her friends a new lease of life.

Growing fruit and veg
From April 2008 to April 2013

Each season has its positives: summer, everything is in full bloom and the days are lighter. Autumn, we can almost feel the anticipation of the farmers at harvest time as they bring in their sheaves. Winter, outside is quiet, and we are cosy inside by the open fire. But spring has to be the best. After a long cold winter, not seeing anyone other than our postman about twice per week, spring is the sign of new life. We can feel Mother Nature's changes, because we have become more sensitive to her elements, because that is all there is. Mallards, drakes and coots return to our pond. At night time we can hear frogs and toads calling to each other, planning where to have their family in our garden. At dusk, we can hear owls calling, badgers fighting and playing, deer calling across the fields, and throughout the day, buzzards circle the tree tops. We can almost feel the pull from Mother Nature to grow something in her garden. The first chance we get, we plant something, anything. Afterall, growing our own produce was one of the reasons for moving here.

*

Our enthusiastic first years of growing fruit and veg.

In the raised beds there are leeks; sweet corn. On the ground level, we grew small curly kale – these continued growing all season, and winter too. The kale leaf is a little tough sometimes and needs to be cooked well, but they still provide us with vitamins. Next to the kale are young runner bean plants, just about to start climbing the cane frames. Under the wire cage, strawberry plants and in the cold frame with the wire lid there is spinach, lettuce and beetroot, with spring onions.

One year, we grew runner beans, and underneath them, planted our pumpkin and squash plants.

This pumpkin plant grew enormous.

We tried in vain to grow cabbage for two years (as with sprouts too), they were either eaten by mice or caterpillars.

Here we planted three rows of six cabbages.

*

This next picture is the greenhouse in between two of our chicken pens. In an ideal place, it catches the sunshine all day long – it also gets very hot, and sometimes we need to provide shade for plants in the form of dense netting. Here we grew tomatoes to each side, and also in large plant pots.

We brought our small curly kale inside to protect them from being eaten by the caterpillars.

In the left-hand corner are yellow courgettes – these are tasty when roasted in the oven with other vegetables, like tomatoes. We also grew lettuce and spring onions in buckets, as well as other locations around the garden.

*

Rows of garlic bulbs - these are really easy to grow:

Although 2012 was a poor year with little sunshine and too much rain, and the bulbs didn't grow very big. Basically, each December we buy a couple large garlic bulbs from a grocers or supermarket, then we break apart the segments and plant them separately. By spring of the following year, they are growing really well into full new bulbs. We usually harvest them around August time by gently lifting them up with a garden fork and hanging them to dry in the greenhouse, to be used in our kitchen and for the chicken's water bowls outside. (Also, I think it is a great feeling to see new growth popping out of the raised soil beds during the depths of winter -for me it's a sign, spring is not so far away.):

*

In the next picture you can see our strawberries – this was early spring 2012 (strawberries loved all the rain, they grew in abundance)...

Frank built the cage using wooden posts, canes and plant pots. We used cheap garden netting – it worked well, and using dark green garden wire, we stretched and fixed it to the frame. In the background of that picture is another fruit cage – Frank made this one in the same way for our raspberries, redcurrant and blackcurrant.

*

Green courgettes have always grown well for us:

However, in our experience, over the past few years, they do not like too much damp or cold. During the damp weather of 2012, they developed mould. We really needed a little more sunshine. In the past, we have grown them in greenhouses and in the raised soil beds outside. In both cases, they flourished. The problem is, neither of us really like green courgettes unless they are disguised in something, like stews, or courgette cake.

*

The less said about cucumbers, the better:

We still have a lot to learn about how to grow cucumbers!

*

This next picture is our proud achievement at growing onions:

It took us two seasonal attempts to get onions to grow large enough and without any rot, but we finally grew enough to hang them up in our under stairs pantry. Every visitor got a peek at our onions, our proud achievements!

*

We haven't quite figured out this next one:

After three attempts of trying to grow sweetcorn, we stopped – it's much easier to buy them from the supermarket. The largest cobs we grew were around three inches long by around one inch in diameter – also, ours tasted peculiar.

*

Rhubarb grows in abundance under our apple tree:

In partial shade, the soil is damp here too. Our rhubarb likes damp and shade.

*

We grew only a small amount of white radish (the bunch on the next photograph, to the side of our garlic bulbs) to see what they tasted like with a salad:

Honeysuckle Cottage's spring onions, spinach leaves and lettuce (no picture available), they passed Frank's approval!

*

Carrots are best grown above ground level, so we had an idea - why not grow them in one of our old dustbins:

So far, so good - the problem is, we picked them a little too early and they tasted awful:

*

We absolutely love tomatoes, all varieties. They are very easy to grow, and the results are rewarding:

We have grown these in the greenhouse, in large plant pots, and outside:

*

Frank and I don't use Chilli and peppers very often:

But I found an interesting way to store them for longer – threaded onto a long cotton string and hung from a beam in the kitchen to dry. It works a treat, and whenever we wanted to add a little spice to a meal, there they were.

*

To say neither of us had mowed a lawn or planted a bulb before we moved to Lincolnshire, we certainly gained experience. Growing fruit and vegetables has proved very rewarding and satisfying. Our learning continues...

Queen of our garden
Saturday 15th February 2014 at 3.45 a.m.

The stormy weather has wreaked havoc with people and places over past few months. However, in our character countryside cottage we have remained thankful, safe and warm. Watching from a distance, the wind, sea and snow brought change. Throughout the United Kingdom and further afield it challenged anyone's notion of weather we once called normal.

Jack barks during the night if there are badgers in our garden. He soon quietens down again and goes back to sleep. But this Saturday morning, there were freak hurricane-like winds, and he was persistent, almost howling, so we got out of bed at 3.45 a.m. to go and see what was the matter with him.

Mother Nature even let the weather bring down our Queen of the garden, our Bramley apple tree. The forty footer whom we met on the first day after our move. The tree we both climbed to rescue our cat. The over one-hundred-year-old giant, with a bench at her base, a front row seat at the open countryside. The tree who brought apples weighing as much as a pound a piece: Maybe Mother Nature decided it was time for a change. 'Frank and Sheila have finished their renovation, let's give 'em something else to do now!' Perhaps she thought we needed another challenge to test our character. But whatever it was, a giant monument now lay across our garden and each time we opened our cottage door, we saw her face.

As she lay resting across the garden, miraculously an old stump from our bay leaf tree broke her fall and prevented further damage. This time, even with help from tree surgeons or tree whisperers, we couldn't pick her up and make everything better...

It took us around two months to burn, recycle or compost her remains:

Who would think it possible to cry over a tree? We loved our Bramley, Queen of the garden.

An old railway sleeper as a bench...

...Queen of our garden could see for miles.

And so to finish...
May 2015

Frank calls it strength and resolve, I call it 'true faith in God'. Frank and I have done our best to keep stable and level minds throughout the past seven years, although I did wobble emotionally for the first couple of years and started to write books to help me get through the journey. Frank calls it sticking my head in the sand. I call it coping. So, if that means developing an imaginary world and inventing characters who end up in a fictitious, but published book, then so be it. That is not such a bad outcome, is it? It may seem a little whacky, but hey, all this would have driven anyone nutty, including the physically fit too. When I take the rose-tinted glasses from my face, the financial, physical and emotional reality blinds me and so they quickly go back in place as I put my head down and write another story.

Maggie took a little longer to accept the choices we made, but she soon came to realise we always had her best interests at heart. She had just finished high school when we first moved to Lincolnshire; already about to enter a new, big wide world by going to college or getting a job. It just so happened that her new life would really be a new start somewhere completely different.

Over the past few years Maggie has managed to go to college, get a part-time job, leave college, get a full-time job, and move out and live on her own, and now she lives with her partner. She has a good, well-paid job and lives close to her friends and work. She is also within easy reach of many return visits to Honeysuckle Cottage.

I asked Maggie what she thought about the experience of living here and whether she would go back and change anything. After a few moments' silence, she looked me in the eye and said, 'No, Mum, I like it here. Mum, I understand why you did it, I would have done the same if I had kids.' She knew we were only trying to give her healthier opportunities. One thing she did say was, 'Why on earth did you have to buy 'that' house, Mum?' I replied, 'Well, do you think we bought a renovation project on purpose? I don't think so.'

I would offer one piece of advice to anyone with a family who is considering a move to the countryside for a better lifestyle. The idea is good but, to us and in hindsight, once a teenage townie, always a teenage townie. I imagine most children, unless quite young, will more than probably get bored and want to stop inside and watch TV all day and play on their mobile phone or computer. The fresh vegetables you may lovingly grow (even though you try to involve your teenager in the process) will probably not be eaten because they are considered strange, being dug up from the ground and not taken out of a cellophane packet from the supermarket. And eggs – well, as soon as they discover they come from the same orifice as hen poo, you may as well buy those in too because no teenager is going to eat fresh healthy eggs from your own stock unless they are disguised in a cardboard egg box. That was our experience – yours may be different.

Frank never ever stopped working. If he wasn't chopping down trees in the snow and ice, he was re-building something in the house. This was not through choice either; he was doing his best to turn the cottage into our home – a place where we could eventually feel settled.

Frank does have a bit of an expressive tendency and if he has something to say, he speaks up, or should I say, shouts it, whatever he has to say – with whomever or wherever – you know what I mean? So, when I hear him shout from the top of our ladder with his arms outstretched in the pouring rain, 'WHY DOES NOBODY EVER LISTEN TO ME? I CAN'T DO THIS ANY MORE – THERE'S ONLY SO MUCH ONE MAN CAN TAKE – I'VE HAD ENOUGH!', so loud it makes him hoarse and loud enough for the entire village to hear, I know he means it from the bottom of his heart.

We are both very tired and much like plasticine – moulded within the renovations and work of Honeysuckle Cottage. When we first moved here and Frank was juggling working in Leeds for most of the week, he would often mention how I acted strangely, almost as if I had become possessed by the cottage, Frank recognised this change in me, probably because he was still half living back in Yorkshire. It must have seemed odd, but once we found him work here in Lincolnshire, he too settled into the rural atmosphere – he too became Honeysuckle Cottage. Now, we feel like we have both become a part of our home, our environment, because we are nearly there and almost complete.

To Frank and me, apart from all the work, it was certainly like a dream come true. In Frank's mind, I think it was like his worst nightmare. He was not as naive as me and certainly understood all the work which needed to be done. I felt sorry for him. Sometimes I wish he could have had more naivety and innocence about the situation to get him through because it certainly helped me cope, although he did have faith, strength and resolve when it came to his abilities and any work in progress.

In the early days, and during the night on wet and windy evenings, because our room was so draughty, both Frank and I could feel the cold right through to our bones, even though we had a feather duvet, hats, gloves and scarves. It was very different living in an old cottage to a modern home. For the first two winters, the wind might as well have been blowing straight through the window whilst we held onto our blankets. Just like a scene from the Wizard of Oz when the hurricane came, only we tried to sleep through it and our house stayed put – although for the feelings we had, we could have been flying.

So far as friends are concerned, we kept in contact with people who we had spent time with whilst doing our psychotherapy studies and friends from a women's charity where I used to volunteer. But our renovation work soon took over and contact dwindled in the process.

Mum and Dad called a handful of times. I remember feeling overwhelmed because they were coming - I wanted the cottage to be perfect. They had not been able to visit often because nanna's health was deteriorating and mum struggles with her mobility. So I knew it was a long trek for them to take. However, when they arrived, we had ready lots of home-made cakes, chutney and jam, with gifts from our garden – the cottage was as perfect as could be, with candles lit and the fire glowing to fill the air with warmth.

Frank kept in contact with his family and colleagues from work in Yorkshire and one or two friends in his personal life. In fact, there was a lovely couple we promised to invite once we were a little more sorted out. It was wonderful to have someone visit and stay with us for a while after being alone in this place for so long and after having little contact with anyone.

For the first couple of years we even returned to Yorkshire to the regular New Year Pantomime at a Harrogate theatre with Frank's old work colleagues. I think Frank really enjoyed the social contact, but again renovation work took precedence and even this came to an end.

Aside from all the work, we have met many interesting and friendly people. I remember when we first moved here, one of our neighbours, whilst we were chatting on Longs Lane, kept saying whilst looking intermittently into the air, 'Oh look there's an owl, there's a hawk', and then, pointing to the fields, 'look a pheasant and a hare!'. We laughed at him when he said he counted how many hares there were each morning in the field and reported the figures to their appreciation society. Our thoughts: 'Yes, we're from the city, but not that gullible'. Well, now we know it's true - we too are now just as strange as our neighbours once seemed – we also appreciate the many hares, rabbits, badgers, sparrows, and pigeons and other creatures who visit our surroundings. When we go to visit our relatives in Leeds and Wakefield, we feel overwhelmed by the smells of fumes and all the built-up areas. People seem rude and ill-mannered because they do not want to or haven't the time to stop and talk. Gosh, if we spoke to a stranger passing in the street they would probably ring the police! Yes, we have changed and have left a lot of our old ways behind, including our sadly missed family and friends. We have become close to nature and truly appreciate the world in which we live. In Mother Nature's garden, where we reside, we see new life...growth...death and new life again and again. It is a natural process, we can't stop it, and we have learned to live here with it instead.

Apart from forgetting how to string a few words together and be sociable, both of us being in constant arthritic pain and my favourite clothing items being my wellington boots and an old muddy fleece, we continue our endeavours to try and live as sane a life as possible.

I swapped my bungalow in Leeds and Frank swapped his modern town house in Wakefield for a windy cottage and we have both paid for it with many different types of physical, emotional and spiritual tests. However, who wouldn't do it? It was our dream, a picture we saw on a Royal Albert plate, and together, with effort and planning, we made our dream come true:

3rd August 2015 – With our breakfast on the patio, Frank and I sat on our two patio chairs overlooking Honeysuckle Cottage and our garden. Listening to the birds and enjoying the stillness after a short rain shower, Frank reached over to take my hand and put it on his lap. He wrapped his other arm around my shoulders and pulled me closer. 'My love, Sheila, my love.'

'I love you too Frank, you did it, you know?'

'No, we did it, we got through – this is our home now.'

There is nothing more to say.

Pros and cons

June 2016

What do we love about our home?

(1) The peace and quiet with no neighbours for around a quarter of a mile.

(2) The animals and birds who visit our garden: badgers, foxes, deer, pigeons, pheasants, stoats, weasels, owls; need I go on?

(3) The clean and fresh air, like no other.

(4) The character of our cottage, with no rooms, no walls, nothing the same. All the floors slope at a different angle and the bedroom slopes downward towards the window by about eight inches.

(5) Sitting in the living room each evening on our antique brown leather chesterfield settee with a thick blanket wrapped around us watching the TV and drinking cocoa.

(6) Sitting in the conservatory on a sunny winter afternoon, watching birds visit their feeders and feeling like we are sitting in the garden – only we are warmer.

(7) Our lovely country pine fitted kitchen.

(8) The massive six-foot original cast iron bath.

(9) The powerful shower upstairs.

(10) The wonderful flush of our downstairs toilet!

(11) The opportunity to grow our own fruit and vegetables.

(12) The opportunity to keep hens and ducks.

(13) Our quaint pieces of furniture, like an old ship's candle lantern and a sixteenth century dark oak cupboard.

(14) Discovering new plants and flowers in our garden.

(15) All the things we have learned about DIY maintenance – like how to make sure our drains run freely and how to clean out our septic tank (and keep it working) and how to check our oil tank and how to compost or recycle our food waste.

(16) The hanging implements from our ceiling beams in the kitchen, like old pans, antique copper jugs and dried bunches of lavender from last year's garden.

(17) The cosy and warm feeling when we get inside our bed, warmed by our fantastic electric blanket, whilst wearing our woollen hats and thick pyjamas – all cuddled up and ready to sleep well.

(18) When the weather is warm enough, sitting outside on the patio and drinking tea from tea cups and eating home-made cakes – whilst enjoying Mother Nature's garden.

(19) Our 'breakfast on the patio' – we do it for real now, in between jobs and in our work clothes and even in January with warm mugs of home-made soup.

(20) Volunteering for the charity shop and the weird and wonderful people we have met since living here.

(21) The local Salvation Army, with their kind and welcoming congregation.

(22) The kind natured people we have met who actually want to chat – even if we don't know them!

(23) The friends we have made.

(24) The surreal 'Vicar of Dibley' style parish council meetings.

(25) The amazement and awe we experience on a clear evening when looking up into the sky at all the stars: The work we have done and the jobs we still need to do just pale into insignificance.

(26) We used to go to Temple Newsome in Leeds to see bats flying around. Now we have them in our garden.

(27) The wonderful opportunity to live close to nature.

(28) The electrifying whoosh of swans as they fly over our cottage.

(29) The 'as if someone has just cracked a joke' quack that a group of ducks make each evening whilst settling on the pond.

What do we dislike about our home?

(1) It feels like the 'Forth Road Bridge' – there is always work to be done.

(2) The countryside gets so muddy – I think I might now have a phobia about mud (amongst other things, insects being one of them).

(3) The unbelievable number of different insects we discover trying to live with us, in our home!

(4) Keeping the big brown country rats under control after the harvest each year.

(5) Our lack of social life and loss of contact with old friends back in Yorkshire.

(6) The financial commitment and having no spare money.

(7) Originally, we didn't intend buying a renovation, it just happened to turn out that way. We probably paid too much for Honeysuckle Cottage simply because the sun was shining and birds were singing on viewing day.

(8) The fact that we have had to undo and redo lots of things in our home to make it habitable.

(9) The feeling of being imprisoned here with all the work and the huge bills, but with strength, resolve and stubborn minds, we stayed and worked at making it easier.

(10) The atmosphere of tension when Frank got home from work exhausted when he had to continue renovating whilst always thinking about how to earn more money just to keep this roof over our heads.

(11) The physical pain. Frank's joints ache from all the work he has put into this constant and ongoing project. I have arthritic pain and some days, I can't move my body to turn over in bed. It's much like the after effects of going camping in the frost and rain. We most probably took on too much and if it wasn't for this writing this book, I don't know where I would be – in hospital I guess. Frank, well he shouts a lot more than he used to do – not at me but at this house and all the work. However, when the sun shines in our Garden of Eden, I often see a smile creep across Frank's face.

(12) Although we keep in regular contact, I miss my family in Leeds.

A misty morning.

My thank you prayer
October 2016

Dear God,

Thank you – thank you so much for helping me find the strength to get through this transition. Thank you for Frank and all the hard work he has endured to get us to this place. Thank you for Maggie and for helping her understand that through all this woodworm and rising damp, we still love her – even though lots of times we couldn't be there as much as we would have liked to have been.

Thank you, Lord, for helping us to turn this house into a home and get through it all in one piece.

Thank you for making us stronger.

And Amen.

Our Favourite home-made recipes
Apple crumble

Apples should be falling from the trees around late September onwards and Bramley's are a good choice for this recipe. This crumble is especially for those cooler autumn months when winter is creeping through the doorways. There is nothing quite like a comfort crumble with lashings of custard.

Take four large apples from the garden. Peel and slice them and add brown sugar to taste (I prefer to use a good quality brown sugar because it adds to the flavour), along with a quarter teaspoon of mixed spice with cinnamon and nutmeg. Place them in a pan with a spoonful or two of water and warm gently at a low heat until slightly soft. Meanwhile, take two ounces of wholewheat plain flour and two ounces of ordinary plain flour and rub in two ounces of butter. Then put in a mixture of oats with wheat germ and oat bran weighing one ounce and add one ounce of brown sugar. (We always have oats, wheatgerm and oat bran in our kitchen cupboards because these are the ingredients for our hot porridge each and every morning, with a few blackberries or whatever fruit is growing in the garden at the time – it is supposed to be good for your heart and certainly provides us with energy for the day.) Place the crumble mixture on top of the apple in an oval glass ovenproof dish and bake at around 160 degrees for around twenty to thirty minutes until you can see the apple bubbling through the glass at the bottom and the crumble is golden brown.

Leave to cool for ten minutes and then serve with a rich fresh thick cream or warm custard. If you have both, add a little cream to the custard, it tastes lovely.

Broccoli Soup

This is one of Maggie's favourites. We always had trouble getting Maggie to eat her greens, especially the ones grown here

at Honeysuckle Cottage, but this soup was just about passable for a growing teenager.

If you have boiled vegetables for dinner, save the water you cooked them in and keep it in the fridge – no more than twenty-four hours though. Then you can use it with the stock for extra vitamins and flavour for the soup. Peel and chop three large boiling potatoes from the garden and one large home-grown onion. Take two large heads of broccoli and chop them quite small, around quarter inch pieces. Melt a teaspoon of butter in a large saucepan and add the potatoes, onion and a little sea salt with black pepper to taste. Gently sweat them for around ten minutes. Then add the chopped broccoli for another five minutes. Meanwhile, heat up the vegetable water from the fridge and add either one vegetable stock cube or one chicken stock cube – whichever you prefer. Boil together all the ingredients without a lid until soft and then use a hand blender for a few seconds to make them into a chunky soup. Add a few drops of fresh cream to taste.

If you want you can add a slice of toasted granary or wholemeal bread from the local bakery (the fresher, the better). Toast on both sides and then butter, sprinkle with a thick layer of parmesan and toast again for a few minutes until golden brown. This recipe has Maggie's seal of approval. Delicious!

Ginger Cake

This cake has been approved by my friends at the charity shop, our local farmer, Ben and John from the telephone company and the electrician who fitted the badger-friendly lighting outside our cottage.

This recipe is enough for a 2 lb lined loaf tin.

Take four ounces of good quality brown granulated sugar, three ounces of butter, three tablespoons of golden syrup and three tablespoons of black treacle and heat gently, stirring occasionally, until the butter has melted and the sugar has dissolved. Allow to cool.

Mix one large free-range egg or one duck egg (duck eggs are brilliant for baking and add a really nice texture to cakes) with seven tablespoons of cold semi-skimmed milk and a good-sized tablespoon of grated fresh root ginger.

Mix eight ounces of plain flour, a pinch of salt, two teaspoons of ground ginger, one teaspoon of ground cinnamon and one and a half teaspoons of baking powder. Add the dry ingredients to the cool syrup mixture and then gradually add the egg mixture whilst stirring slowly with a wooden spoon. Make sure all the ingredients are mixed well together and tip into the loaf tin. Bake at a low temperature of 150–160 degrees for around one to one and a half hours. (A good tip to test and see if your cake is ready is to use a skewer and insert it gently into the middle. If the skewer comes out clean and free from sticky cake mixture, the cake is ready to be removed from the oven.) I find this cake is best left to cool and to settle for at least twenty-four hours before cutting and keeps for around ten days, covered. It also freezes well and I have found this to bring out more of the flavour too.

Nanna's Cake

Nanna doesn't make cakes any more, but years ago she taught my brother and I how to bake them. We all love Nanna so very much and are so very grateful for everything she taught us.

I used to have trouble getting my cake recipes to work; somehow the ingredients didn't seem to blend well enough and I would miss out some essential part, until Nanna gave me this simple recipe and it seems to work just perfectly every time.

I have written this recipe in the exact way Nanna spoke it to me:

'Get out your balancing scales – all these ingredients must be equal. Replace the weights with the eggs and put an equal amount of flour of the raising type, along with butter and sugar too. Now, add one small teaspoon of *baker's powder and one tablespoon of **ground-up almonds – mix it all together with a large wooden spoon of warm water. Now you are ready to bake, my dear – in your usual cake tin, at a low, gentle heat. Go out now, share and enjoy the fruits of your labour. Remember, if ever a day goes by when I don't say I love you, know that I always do.'

*I presumed Nanna was referring to baking powder.

** These are just normal ground almonds.

Mum's Raspberry Buns

This is a 1960s' school home economics recipe Mum taught me: thank you Mum. I can honestly say these can be fresh baked and out with a cup of tea by the time the small talk has finished around the dining table. They are ideal to make in a rush, full of flavour and very moreish. This is a tried and tested and easy to make recipe. Now we have our own home-grown raspberries, we can add our own jam to it too.

(To make our raspberry jam: pick eight ounces of raspberries from the garden – blackberries are good too. Use the juice from half a lemon and four ounces of good quality sugar. At a gentle heat, mix together the ingredients and keep on a medium heat whilst stirring continuously for about five minutes, or until the sugar has dissolved and the mixture has thickened slightly. Put on one side to cool a little.)

Take eight ounces of self-raising flour with a pinch of salt and rub in three ounces of butter to resemble breadcrumbs. Mix in four ounces of caster sugar and use enough milk to make the mixture bind into a dough. It usually takes around two to three tablespoons of milk to achieve this consistency. Then turn onto a lightly floured surface, and after kneading lightly, divide into eight evenly sized balls. Make a hole in the centre of each with your thumb and put a couple of teaspoons of jam in the middle.

Sprinkle with a little brown sugar and bake at about 180 degrees for around fifteen to twenty minutes. Be aware: the jam can be very hot and burn straight from the oven.

Lemon Cake

This cake has a wonderful moist refreshing taste. We have it with tea served in cups and saucers whilst sitting on our patio on a spring day to celebrate all the new life growing in our garden.

Cream together seven ounces of butter and seven ounces of caster sugar until pale and fluffy. Beat in three large free-range eggs or two duck eggs along with five ounces of self-raising flour and two ounces of corn flour. Add half a teaspoon of baking powder and the zest of one finely grated unwaxed lemon. Mix well.

Bake in a lined 2 lb loaf tin at 160 degrees for around thirty minutes. Allow to cool.

Mix six ounces of icing sugar with the juice of the lemon and pour over the top of the lemon cake. Or mix the juice of the lemon with a little sugar and spoon it over the warm cake. When cool, dust with icing sugar. Slice and serve with tea.

Tangy apple chutney

This is a really tasty and tangy recipe to use up more apples from the garden. Peel, core and chop 2 lb of windfall apples and two medium onions. Put them all in a large heavy-bottomed pan (not aluminium because it alters the taste) with two teaspoons of paprika and cook gently for five minutes until everything starts to soften. Split six cardamom pods and crush the seeds. Peel and chop a generous two-inch piece of fresh ginger. Add these ingredients to the pan along with fifteen fluid ounces of cider vinegar and stir well for about five minutes. Chop one small packet of dried cranberries and one small packet of dried apricots and add along with eleven ounces of brown sugar and simmer for around fifteen to twenty minutes or until thick and pulpy. Spoon into warm sterilised jars. Keep for around two months before opening. This allows the flavour to mature.

(This is only my experience, but I find putting the chutney into hot sterilised jars, being careful not to burn myself, works better for a good seal. As the air cools down in the closed jars, the lid should seal tighter. This worked for us and they lasted a good few months stored in our understairs pantry.)

Elderflower cordial

Both Frank and I just love the fragrant taste of this, particularly served as a long chilled drink on a hot summer's day, especially as a mix with ginger wine. (Unfortunately, I haven't a recipe for ginger wine because it is so much easier to go to the local supermarket and purchase some already made. However, maybe one day, when we finish working on Honeysuckle Cottage, we will make some of our own – perhaps whilst writing our next book.)

Take twenty large elderflower heads (remove as many of the large stalks as possible) and shake them gently to get rid of any little bugs. Add to a pan of one and a half litres water and one and a half kilos of caster sugar and a teaspoon of grated rind and all the juice of two large unwaxed lemons.

Add seventy-five grams of citric acid (which can be purchased from your local chemist). Bring to the boil and then add the flower heads and take off the heat. Leave to cool, cover with a lid and stand at room temperature for twenty-hours. Then, drain the cordial through a muslin cloth and into very clean bottles with tightly fitting caps. Store in a cool place and serve chilled.

There's always time for baking!

About the author

Sheila Douthwaite started writing in 2007 to help her cope with the transition of moving from a modern lifestyle in Leeds to a countryside cottage in rural Lincolnshire. This book is a recorded trophy for all their hard work.

Inspired by the natural environment, the author also invented characters and wrote a make-believe story based around their cottage and its gardens. The main character, Narnah Buntwinkle, overcomes many obstacles. For more information about Narnah's healing journey, please visit www.nuttynarrator.blogspot.com.

Articles about the author's writing projects have been published in The Writing Magazine, The Lincolnshire Life Magazine, The Lincolnshire Echo Newspaper, The Lincolnshire Poacher, Skegness Standard and Louth Leader Newspaper.

Breakfast on the Patio is available through public libraries, to purchase through the internet, and available to order through most bookstores on the high street.

For more information, please visit Frank and Sheila's blog at www.busycornerbooks.blogspot.co.uk or their website at www.busycornerbooks.com.

Our Breakfast on the Patio.

November 2016 Update

Dear Friends,

Firstly, we would like to thank everyone who purchased a copy of Breakfast on the Patio. Also for your kind and encouraging words about our ongoing renovation journey, with special thanks to our author friend, Carol Arnall.

This book has remained on Amazon Kindle's best sellers list in Home Repair for over 2 years, often at No.1! With Amazon's kind permission, we can call our very own escape to the country, a 'Bestseller'!

Frank and I made our dream come true with hard work and determination: we made it work, thank goodness. However, both of us needed a rest. In July 2016 we sold our beautiful Honeysuckle Cottage, packed up our belongings, re-homed our much-loved hens, moved out, and settled into a bungalow in a pretty village near Louth. Although it was difficult to say goodbye, life *is* much easier now. Frank and I had a wonderful opportunity to be close-up to Mother Nature. Those memories will remain with us forever.

Sending you love and prayers,
Frank & Sheila.